SKILLS For SUCCESS

with

Office 2010 Web Apps

GETTING STARTED

SKILLS For SUCCESS

with

Office 2010 Web Apps

GETTING STARTED

REBECCA LAWSON | KRIS TOWNSEND

PEARSON

Boston Columbus Indianapolis New York San Francisco Upper Saddle River
Amsterdam Cape Town Dubai London Madrid Milan Munich Paris Montréal Toronto
Delhi Mexico City São Paulo Sydney Hong Kong Seoul Singapore Taipei Tokyo

Library of Congress Cataloging-in-Publication Data
Lawson, Rebecca.
Skills for success with office 2010 web apps getting started / Lawson, Townsend.
p. cm. — (Skills for success)
Includes bibliographical references and index.
ISBN-13: 978-0-13-255004-8
ISBN-10: 0-13-255004-0
1. Microsoft Office. 2. Business--Computer programs. 3. Application software. I. Townsend, Kris. II. Title.
HF5548.4.M525L39 2013
006.7'8—dc23 2011039183

Editor in Chief: *Michael Payne*
Product Development Manager: *Laura Burgess*
Senior Editorial Project Manager: *Meghan Bisi and Kerri Tomasso*
Editorial Assistant: *Carly Prakapas*
Development Editor: *Vonda Keator*
VP/Director of Business & Technology Marketing: *Patrice Lumumba Jones*
Marketing Coordinator: *Susan Osterlitz*
Marketing Assistant: *Darshika Vyas*
Associate Managing Editor: *Camille Trentacoste*
Senior Production Project Manager: *Rhonda Aversa*
Senior Operation Manager/Site Lead: *Nick Sklitsis*
IT Procurement Lead: *Natacha Moore*
Operations Specialist: *Maura Zaldivar-Garcia*
Senior Art Director: *Jonathan Boylan*
Text and Cover Designer: *Jonathan Boylan*
Director of Digital Development: *Zara Wanlass*
Editor—Digial Learning & Assessment: *Paul Gentile*
Director of Media Development: *Cathi Profitko*
Senior Media Project Manager, Editorial: *Alana Coles*
Media Project Manager, Production: *John Cassar*
Full-Service Project Management: *Electronic Publishing Services Inc., NYC*
Full-Service Project Manager: *Melinda Durham*
Composition: *Jouve*
Printer/Binder: *Quad Graphics/Eusey Press Inc.*
Cover Printer: *Lehigh-Phoenix Color/Hagerstown*
Typeface: *Minion Pro Regular 10.5/12.5*

Credits and acknowledgments borrowed from other sources and reproduced, with permission, in this textbook appear on appropriate page within text.

PEARSON

10 9 8 7 6 5 4 3 2 1
ISBN-13: 978-0-13-255004-8
ISBN-10: 0-13-255004-0

Table of Contents

Contributors

We thank the following people for their hard work and support in making Skills For Success all that it is!

Technical Editors

Lisa Bucki
Cheryl Slavik
Janet Pickard

Reviewers

Laurel Aagard	*Sierra College*
John Alcorcha	*MTI College*
Barry Andrews	*Miami Dade College*
Natalie Andrews	*Sinclair Community College*
Wilma Andrews	*Virginia Commonwealth University School of Business*
Bridget Archer	*Oakton Community College*
Greg Ballinger	*Miami Dade College–Kendall Campus*
Terry Bass	*University of Massachusetts, Lowell*
Rocky Belcher	*Sinclair Community College*
Nannette Bibby	*Miami Dade College–Kendall Campus*
Alisa Brown	*Pulaski Technical College*
Eric Cameron	*Passaic Community College*
Trey Cherry	*Edgecombe Community College*
Kim Childs	*Bethany University*
Pauline Chohonis	*Miami Dade College–Kendall Campus*
Lennie Cooper	*Miami Dade College–North Campus*
Gail Cope	*Sinclair Community College*
Chris Corbin	*Miami Dade College*
Tommi Crawford	*Miami Dade College–Kendall Campus*
Martin Cronlund	*Anne Arundel Community College*
Jennifer Day	*Sinclair Community College*
Ralph De Arazoza	*Miami Dade College–Kendall Campus*
Loorna DeDuluc	*Miami Dade College*
Caroline Delcourt	*Black Hawk College*
Michael Discello	*Pittsburgh Technical Institute*
Kevin Duggan	*Midlands Technical Community College*
Barbara Edington	*St. Francis College*
Donna Ehrhart	*Genesee Community College*
Tushnelda Fernandez	*Miami Dade College*
Arlene Flerchinger	*Chattanooga State Tech Community College*
Hedy Fossenkemper	*Paradise Valley Community College*
Kent Foster	*Winthrop University*
Arlene Franklin	*Bucks County Community College*
George Gabb	*Miami Dade College*
Deb Geoghan	*Bucks County Community College*
Jessica Gilmore	*Highline Community College*
Victor Giol	*Miami Dade College*
Linda Glassburn	*Cuyahoga Community College, West*
Deb Gross	*Ohio State University*
Rachelle Hall	*Glendale Community College*
Marie Hartlein	*Montgomery County Community College*
Diane Hartman	*Utah Valley State College*
Patrick Healy	*Northern Virginia Community College—Woodbridge*
Lindsay Henning	*Yavapai College*
Kermelle Hensley	*Columbus Technical College*
Mary Carole Hollingsworth	*GA Perimeter*
Stacey Gee Hollins	*St. Louis Community College—Meramec*
Joan Ivey	*Lanier Technical College*

Kay Johnston	*Columbia Basin College*
Sally Kaskocsak	*Sinclair Community College*
Hazel Kates	*Miami Dade College*
Charles Kellermann	*Northern Virginia Community College Woodbridge*
John Kidd	*Tarrant County Community College*
Chris Kinnaird	*Miami Dade College–Wolfson Campus*
Kelli Kleindorfer	*American Institute of Business*
Kurt Kominek	*Northeast State Technical Community College*
Dianne Kotokoff	*Lanier Technical College*
Jean Lacoste	*Virginia Tech*
Gene Laughrey	*Northern Oklahoma College*
David Lebron	*Miami Dade College–Wolfson Campus*
Kaiyang Liang	*Miami Dade College*
Linda Lindaman	*Black Hawk College*
Felix Lopez	*Miami Dade College*
Nicki Maines	*Mesa Community College*
Cindy Manning	*Big Sandy Community and Technical College*
Patri Mays	*Paradise Valley Community College*
Sandy McCormack	*Monroe Community College*
Lee McKinley	*GA Perimeter*
Eric Meyer	*Miami Dade College*
Jackie Meyers	*Sinclair Community College*
Kathryn Miller	*Big Sandy Community and Technical College, Pikeville Campus*
Kathy Morris	*University of Alabama, Tuscaloosa*
Linda Moulton	*Montgomery County Community College*
Ryan Murphy	*Sinclair Community College*
Stephanie Murre Wolf	*Moraine Park Technical College*
Jackie Myers	*Sinclair Community College*
Dell Najera	*El Paso Community College, Valle Verde Campus*
Scott Nason	*Rowan Cabarrus Community College*
Paula Neal	*Sinclair Community College*
Eloise Newsome	*Northern Virginia Community College—Woodbridge*
Ellen Orr	*Seminole Community College*
Carol Ottaway	*Chemeketa Community College*
Denise Passero	*Fulton-Montgomery Community College*
Janet Pickard	*Chattanooga State Tech Community College*
Floyd Pittman	*Miami Dade College*
Melissa Prinzing	*Sierra College*
Pat Rahmlow	*Montgomery County Community College*
Kamaljeet Sanghera	*George Mason University*
Teresa Sept	*College of Southern Idaho*
Gary Sibbits	*St. Louis Community College-Meramec*
Janet Siert	*Ellsworth Community College*
Robert Sindt	*Johnson County Community College*
Robert Smolenski	*Delaware County Community College*
Patricia Snyder	*Midlands Technical Community College*
Diane Stark	*Phoenix College*
Linda Stoudemayer	*Lamar Institute of Technology*
Linda Switzer	*Highline Community College*
Margaret Taylor	*College of Southern Nevada*
Martha Taylor	*Sinclair Community College*
Roseann Thomas	*Fayetteville Tech Community College*
Ingrid Thompson-Sellers	*GA Perimeter*
Daniel Thomson	*Keiser University*
Barb Tollinger	*Sinclair Community College*
Cathy Urbanski	*Chandler Gilbert Community College*
Philip Vavalides	*Guilford Technical Community College*
Pete Vetere	*Montgomery County Community College—West Campus*
Asteria Villegas	*Monroe College*
Michael Walton	*Miami Dade College*
Teri Weston	*Harford Community College*
Julie Wheeler	*Sinclair Community College*
Debbie Wood	*Western Piedmont Community College*
Thomas Yip	*Passaic Community College*
Matt Zullo	*Wake Technical Community College*

Instructors - You asked for it so here it is!

A Microsoft® Office textbook that recognizes how students learn today-

Skills for Success

with Office 2010 Web Apps

- **10 x 8.5 Format -** Easy for students to read and type at the same time by simply propping the book up on the desk in front of their monitor
- **Clearly Outlined Skills -** Each skill is presented in a single two-page spread so that students can easily follow along
- **Numbered Steps and Bulleted Text -** Students don't read long paragraphs or text, but they will read information presented concisely

Chapter Introduction - Briefs students on what is important and sets the stage for the project the student will create

File Summary - A quick summary of the files the students need to open and the names of the files they will turn in

Clock - Tells how much time students need to complete the chapter

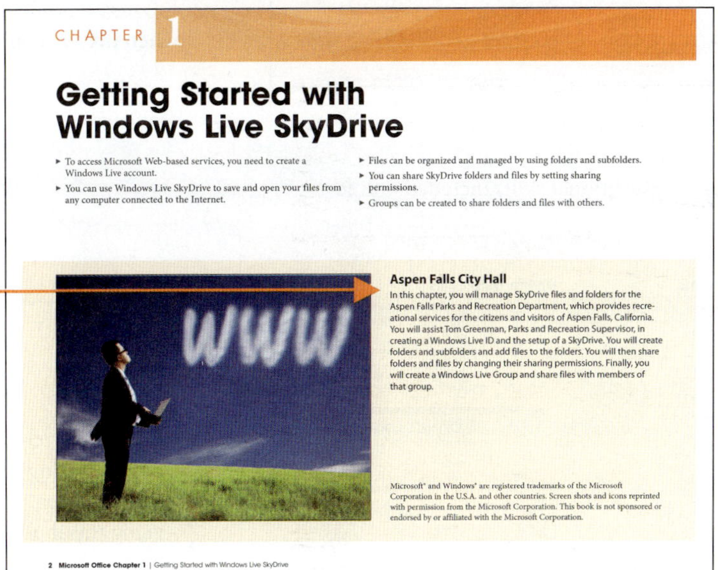

CHAPTER 1

Getting Started with Windows Live SkyDrive

- To access Microsoft Web-based services, you need to create a Windows Live account.
- You can use Windows Live SkyDrive to save and open your files from any computer connected to the Internet.
- Files can be organized and managed by using folders and subfolders.
- You can share SkyDrive folders and files by setting sharing permissions.
- Groups can be created to share folders and files with others.

Aspen Falls City Hall

In this chapter, you will manage SkyDrive files and folders for the Aspen Falls Parks and Recreation Department, which provides recreational services for the citizens and visitors of Aspen Falls, California. You will assist Tom Greenman, Parks and Recreation Supervisor, in creating a Windows Live ID and the setup of a SkyDrive. You will create folders and subfolders and add files to the folders. You will then share folders and files by changing their sharing permissions. Finally, you will create a Windows Live Group and share files with members of that group.

Microsoft® and Windows® are registered trademarks of the Microsoft Corporation in the U.S.A. and other countries. Screen shots and icons reprinted with permission from the Microsoft Corporation. This book is not sponsored or endorsed by or affiliated with the Microsoft Corporation.

2 **Microsoft Office Chapter 1** | Getting Started with Windows Live SkyDrive

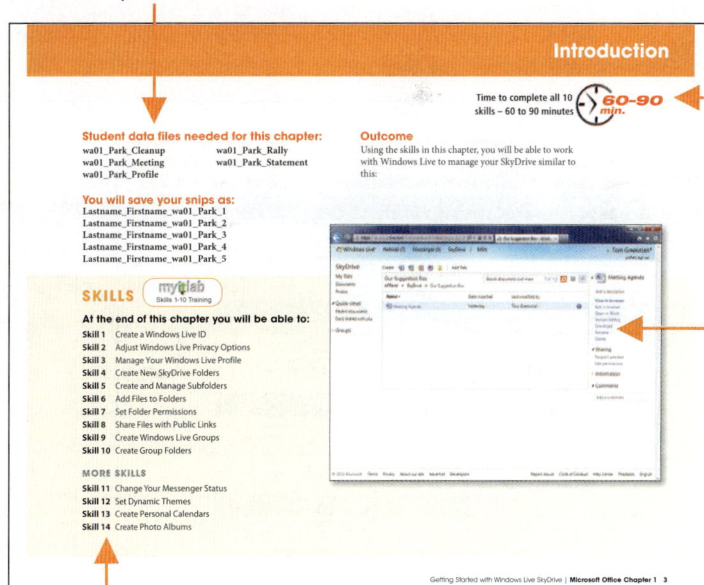

Introduction

Time to complete all 10 skills – 60 to 90 minutes — 60-90 min.

Student data files needed for this chapter:

wa01_Park_Cleanup
wa01_Park_Meeting
wa01_Park_Profile
wa01_Park_Rally
wa01_Park_Statement

You will save your snips as:

Lastname_Firstname_wa01_Park_1
Lastname_Firstname_wa01_Park_2
Lastname_Firstname_wa01_Park_3
Lastname_Firstname_wa01_Park_4
Lastname_Firstname_wa01_Park_5

Outcome

Using the skills in this chapter, you will be able to work with Windows Live to manage your SkyDrive similar to this:

SKILLS myitlab Skills 1-10 Training

At the end of this chapter you will be able to:

Skill 1 Create a Windows Live ID
Skill 2 Adjust Windows Live Privacy Options
Skill 3 Manage Your Windows Live Profile
Skill 4 Create New SkyDrive Folders
Skill 5 Create and Manage Subfolders
Skill 6 Add Files to Folders
Skill 7 Set Folder Permissions
Skill 8 Share Files with Public Links
Skill 9 Create Windows Live Groups
Skill 10 Create Group Folders

MORE SKILLS

Skill 11 Change Your Messenger Status
Skill 12 Set Dynamic Themes
Skill 13 Create Personal Calendars
Skill 14 Create Photo Albums

Getting Started with Windows Live SkyDrive | **Microsoft Office Chapter 1** 3

Sequential Pagination - Saves you and your students time in locating topics and assignments

Skills List - A visual snapshot of what skills they will complete in the chapter

Outcome - Shows students up front what their completed project will look like

Skills for Success

Written for Today's Students – Skills are taught with numbered steps and bulleted text so students are less likely to skip valuable information

Two-Page Spreads – Each skill is presented on a two-page spread to help students keep up their momentum

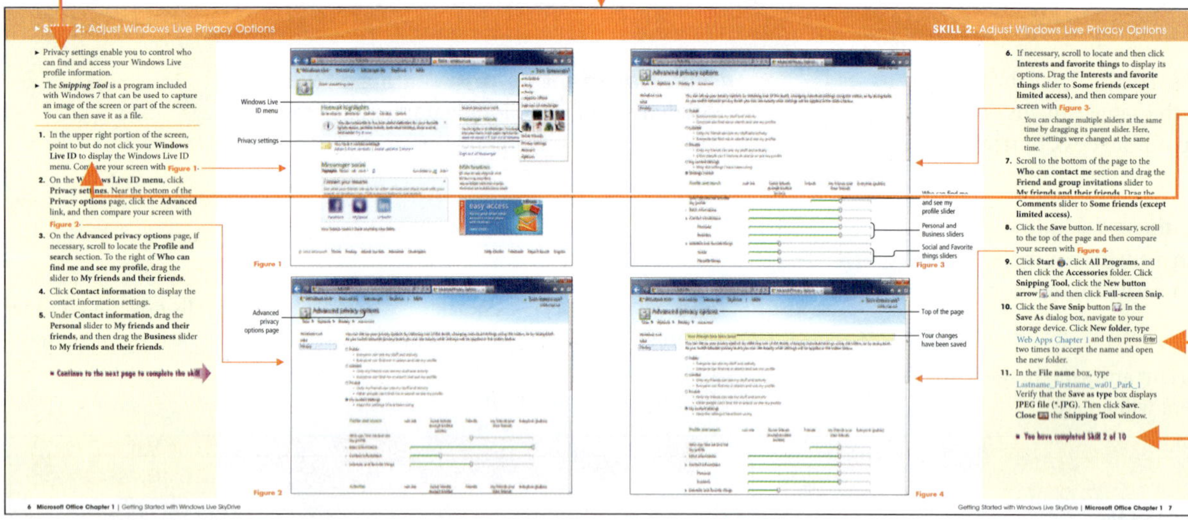

Hands-On – Students start actually working on their skills from Step 1

Colored Text – Clearly shows what a student types

Done! – Students always know when they've completed a skill

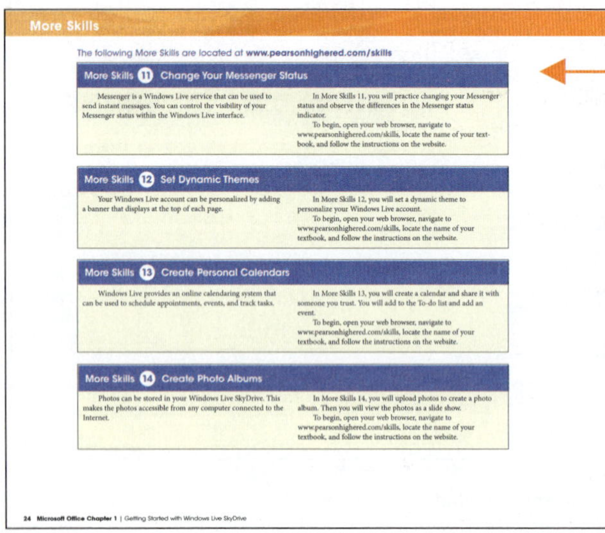

More Skills – Additional skills included online

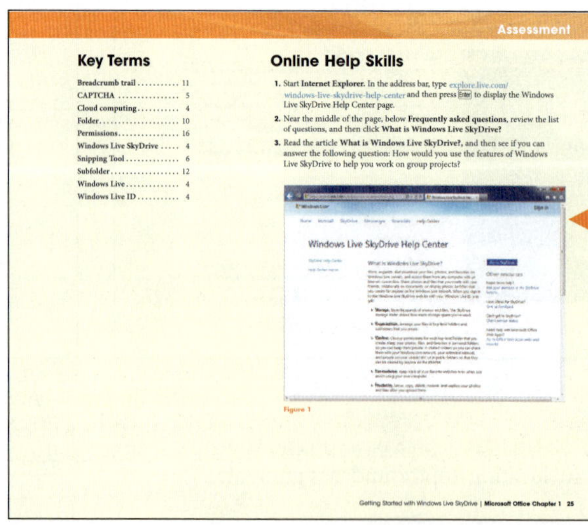

Online Project – Students practice using Microsoft Help online to help prepare them for using the applications on their own

Skills for Success

End-of-Chapter Material – Several levels of assessment so you can assign the material that best fits your students' needs

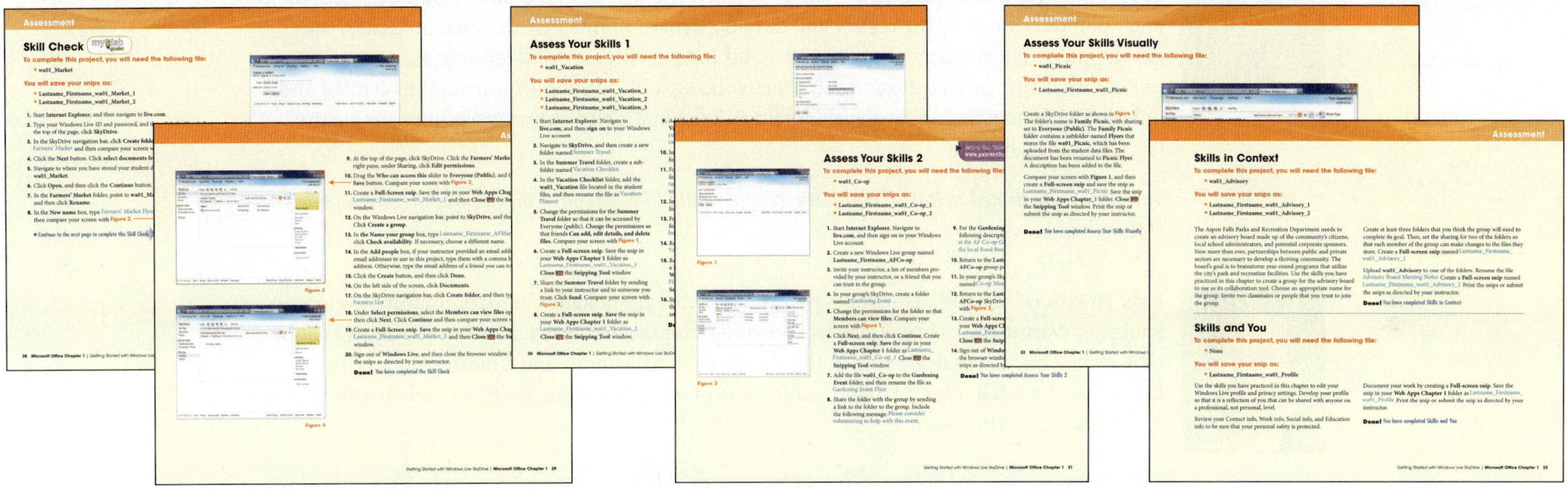

All Instructor materials available on the IRC

Instructor Materials

Instructor's Manual – Teaching tips and additional resources for each chapter

Assignment Sheets – Lists all the assignments for the chapter, you just add in the course information, due dates and points. Providing these to students ensures they will know what is due and when

Scripted Lectures – Classroom lectures prepared for you

Annotated Solution Files – Coupled with the scoring rubrics, these create a grading and scoring system that makes grading so much easier for you

Power Point Lectures – PowerPoint presentations for each chapter

Prepared Exams – Exams for each chapter

Scoring Rubrics – Can be used either by students to check their work or by you as a quick check-off for the items that need to be corrected

Test Bank – Includes a variety of test questions for each chapter

Companion Website – Online content such as the More Skills Projects, Online Study Guide, Glossary, and Student Data Files are all at www.pearsonhighered.com/skills

About the Authors

Rebecca Lawson is a professor in the Computer Information Technologies program at Lansing Community College. She also serves as the Online Faculty Coordinator at the Center for Teaching Excellence at LCC. She is certified in online curriculum quality assurance. Her major areas of interest include the review and development of online instructional materials, the development and assessment of computer and Internet literacy skill levels to facilitate student retention, the use of Web 2.0 and social networking tools to support learning in blended and online environments, and the development and facilitation of online workshops for faculty learning to teach online.

This book is dedicated to Rachel and Katy. Where would I be without your inspiration and support?
—Rebecca Lawson

Kris Townsend is an Information Systems instructor at Spokane Falls Community College in Spokane, Washington. He has also worked as a public school teacher and as a systems analyst. Kris earned bachelor's degrees in both Education and Business, and a master's degree in Education. Kris can often be found outdoors exploring, photographing, and reliving the history of the Pacific Northwest.

This is book is dedicated to the students at Spokane Falls Community College. Their adventures always guide my way.
—Kris Townsend

SKILLS For SUCCESS

with

Office 2010 Web Apps

GETTING STARTED

CHAPTER 1

Getting Started with Windows Live SkyDrive

- To access Microsoft Web-based services, you need to create a Windows Live account.
- You can use Windows Live SkyDrive to save and open your files from any computer connected to the Internet.
- Files can be organized and managed by using folders and subfolders.
- You can share SkyDrive folders and files by setting sharing permissions.
- Groups can be created to share folders and files with others.

Tom Wang/Shutterstock

Aspen Falls City Hall

In this chapter, you will manage SkyDrive files and folders for the Aspen Falls Parks and Recreation Department, which provides recreational services for the citizens and visitors of Aspen Falls, California. You will assist Tom Greenman, Parks and Recreation Supervisor, in creating a Windows Live ID and the setup of a SkyDrive. You will create folders and subfolders and add files to the folders. You will then share folders and files by changing their sharing permissions. Finally, you will create a Windows Live Group and share files with members of that group.

Time to complete all 10 skills – 60 to 90 minutes

60–90 min.

Student data files needed for this chapter:

wa01_Park_Cleanup
wa01_Park_Meeting
wa01_Park_Profile
wa01_Park_Rally
wa01_Park_Statement

You will save your snips as:

Lastname_Firstname_wa01_Park_1
Lastname_Firstname_wa01_Park_2
Lastname_Firstname_wa01_Park_3
Lastname_Firstname_wa01_Park_4
Lastname_Firstname_wa01_Park_5

Outcome

Using the skills in this chapter, you will be able to work with Windows Live to manage your SkyDrive similar to this:

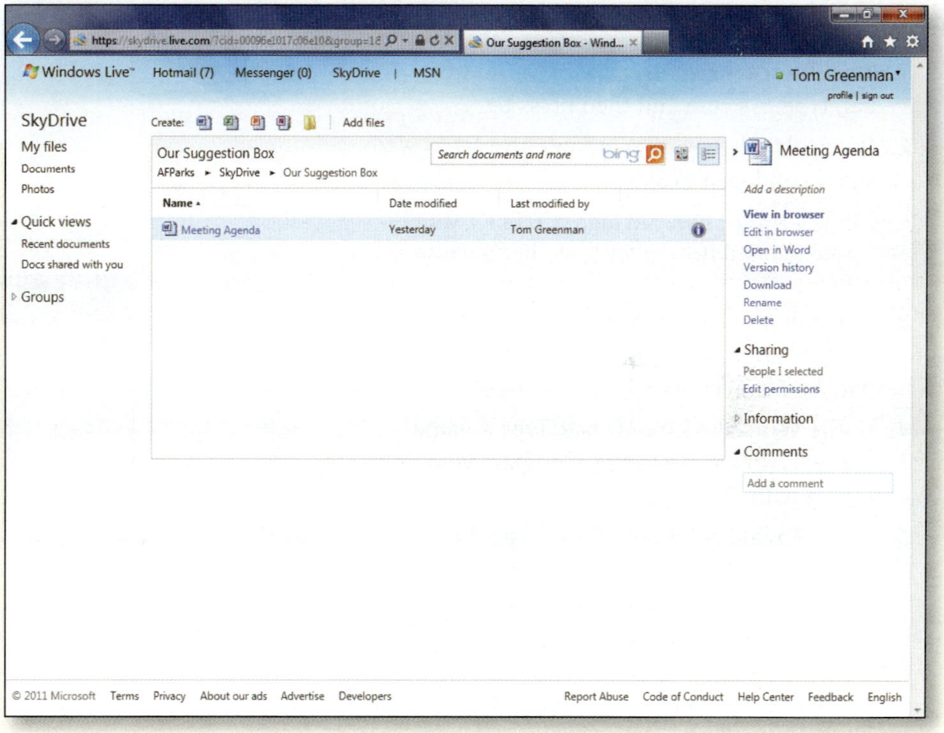

SKILLS

At the end of this chapter you will be able to:

Skill 1 Create a Windows Live ID
Skill 2 Adjust Windows Live Privacy Options
Skill 3 Manage Your Windows Live Profile
Skill 4 Create New SkyDrive Folders
Skill 5 Create and Manage Subfolders
Skill 6 Add Files to Folders
Skill 7 Set Folder Permissions
Skill 8 Share Files with Public Links
Skill 9 Create Windows Live Groups
Skill 10 Create Group Folders

MORE SKILLS

Skill 11 Change Your Messenger Status
Skill 12 Set Dynamic Themes
Skill 13 Create Personal Calendars
Skill 14 Create Photo Albums

- ▸ ***Windows Live*** is a large group of cloud-based technologies including email, social networking, and applications that are accessed through a website that is used for communication, storage of files and folders, and sharing of files and folders.
- ▸ ***Windows Live SkyDrive*** is a Windows Live service used to store, access, and share files and folders.
- ▸ A ***Windows Live ID*** is the email address that is your user name to log on to Windows Live.
- ▸ ***Cloud computing*** is an Internet technology used to store files and to work with programs that are stored in a central location.

1. Start **Internet Explorer**. In the address bar, type live.com and then press Enter.
2. If you already have a Windows Live ID, sign in and skip to Skill 2.

   If you already have a Windows Live ID, your screen may differ slightly from the figures in this book.
3. If you do not have a Windows Live ID, click the **Sign up** button, and then compare your screen with **Figure 1**.
4. In the **Windows Live ID** box, type a name that you would like to use. Compare your screen with **Figure 2**.
5. In the **Create a password** box, type the password you would like to use. Type it once more in the Retype password box.

   As you type, an indicator shows your password strength. A strong password contains 7 to 16 characters and a mix of uppercase and lowercase letters, symbols, and numbers. It does not include commonly used names or words.

■ **Continue to the next page to complete the skill**

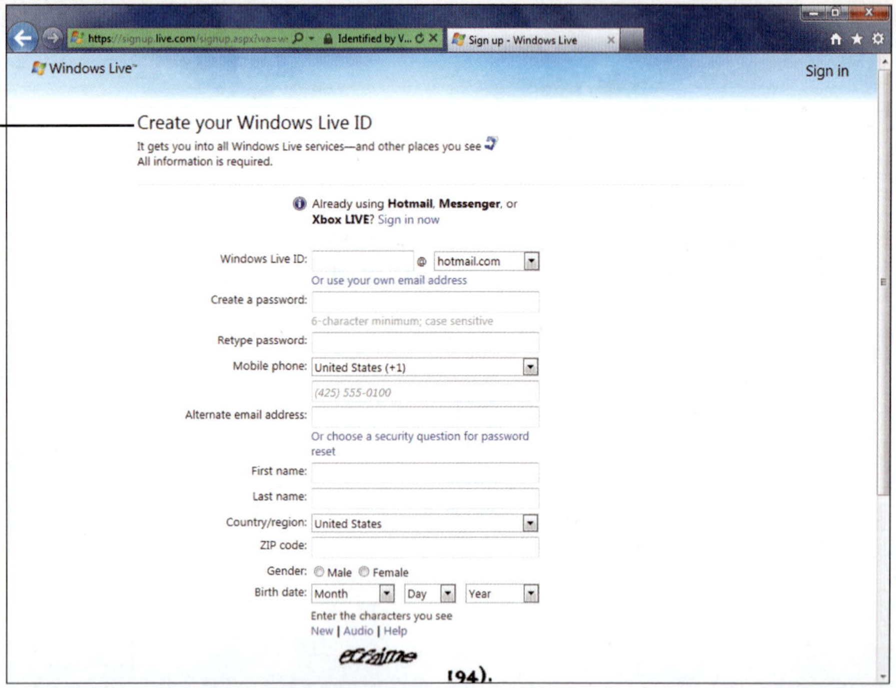

Figure 1

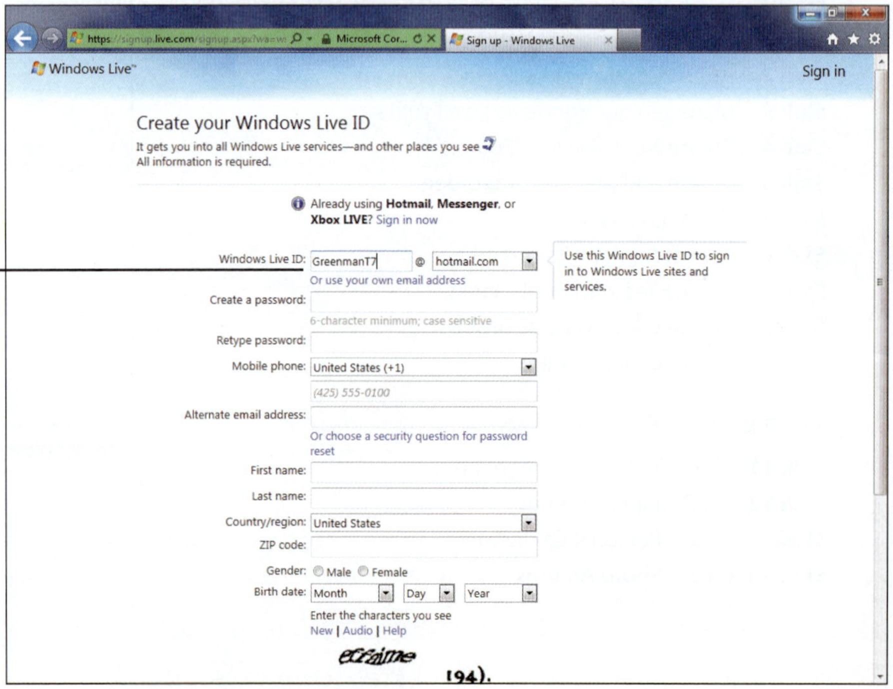

Figure 2

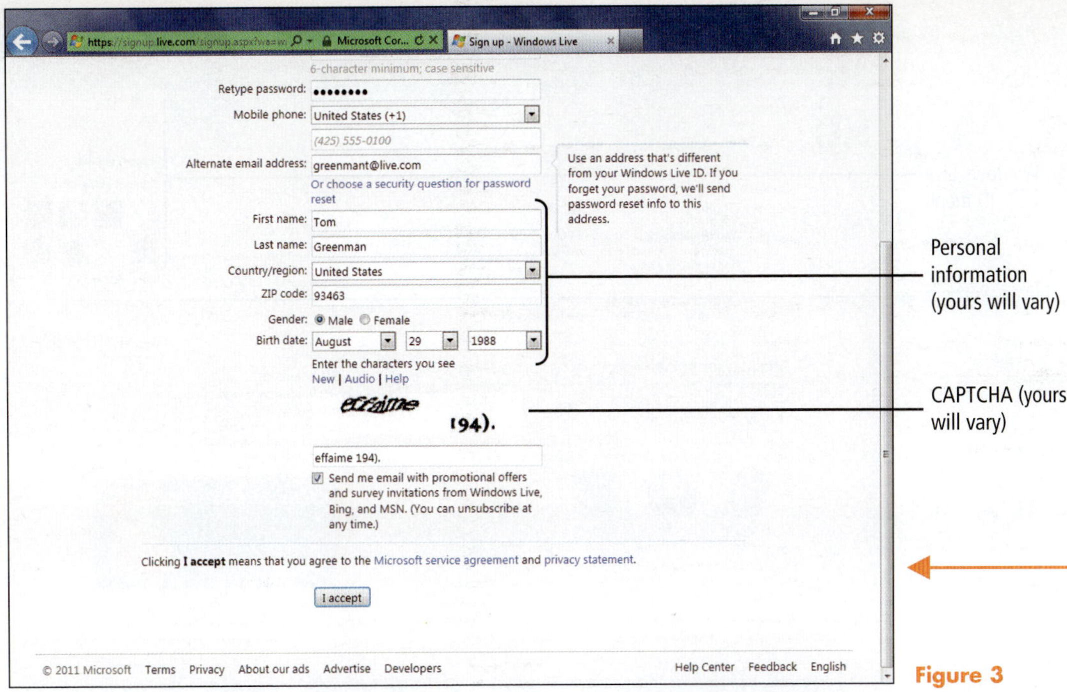

Figure 3

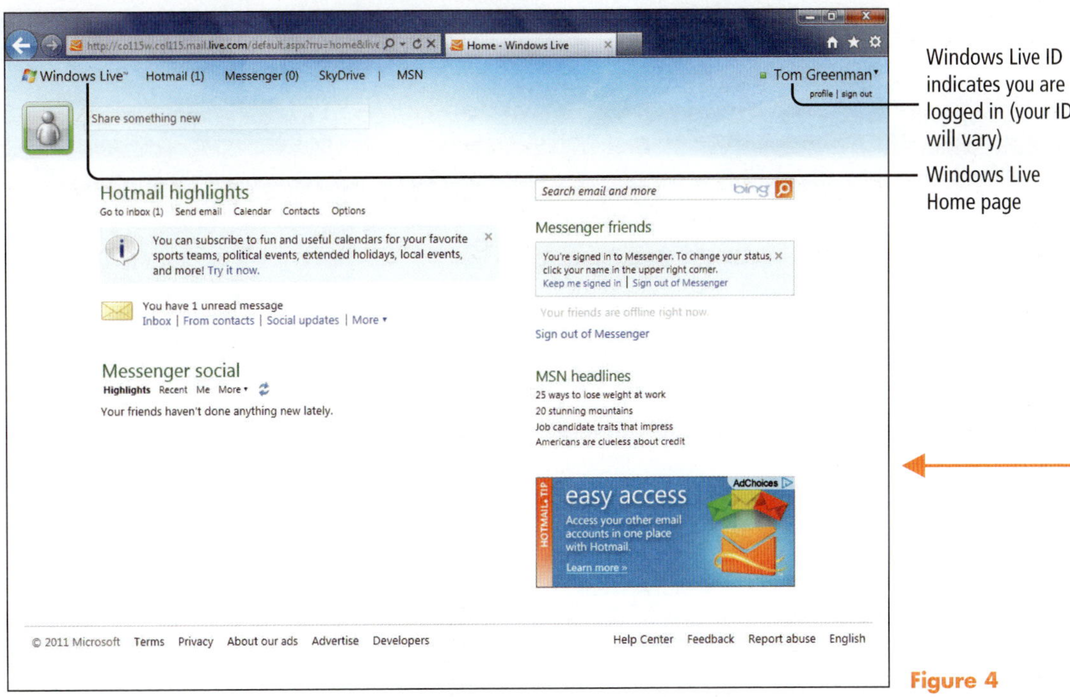

Figure 4

6. In the **Alternate email address** box, type one of your other email addresses. If you do not have an alternate address, click **Or choose a security question for password reset** and then enter a security question and answer.
7. Scroll down on the **Create your Windows Live ID** page, and then type your **First name**, **Last name**, **Country/region**, **State**, and **ZIP code**.
8. To the right of **Gender**, click the appropriate option button. In the **Birth date** boxes, add your month, day, and year.
9. If necessary, scroll to the bottom of the page. In the last box, type the CAPTCHA code that displays on your screen. Compare your screen with **Figure 3**.

   A ***CAPTCHA*** is a test used to ensure that forms are filled in by human beings. They are commonly used to prevent computer programs from automating tasks such as creating Windows Live accounts. Too many automated requests could cause the servers to fail.

10. At the bottom of the page, click the **Microsoft service agreement** link. Read the agreement, and then **Close** the tab to return to the **Create your Windows Live ID** page.
11. Click the **privacy statement** link. Read the statement, and then **Close** the tab.
12. At the bottom of the **Create your Windows Live ID** page, click the **I accept** button, and then compare your screen with **Figure 4**.

   Windows Live web pages are dynamic—they frequently change. For this reason, your screen may display a different page than the one shown in Figure 4.

■ **You have completed Skill 1 of 10**

- Privacy settings enable you to control who can find and access your Windows Live profile information.
- The ***Snipping Tool*** is a program included with Windows 7 that can be used to capture an image of the screen or part of the screen. You can then save it as a file.

1. In the upper right portion of the screen, point to but do not click your **Windows Live ID** to display the Windows Live ID menu. Compare your screen with **Figure 1**.
2. On the **Windows Live ID menu**, click **Privacy settings**. Near the bottom of the **Privacy options** page, click the **Advanced** link, and then compare your screen with **Figure 2**.
3. On the **Advanced privacy options** page, if necessary, scroll to locate the **Profile and search** section. To the right of **Who can find me and see my profile**, drag the slider to **My friends and their friends**.
4. Click **Contact information** to display the contact information settings.
5. Under **Contact information**, drag the **Personal** slider to **My friends and their friends**, and then drag the **Business** slider to **My friends and their friends**.

■ **Continue to the next page to complete the skill**

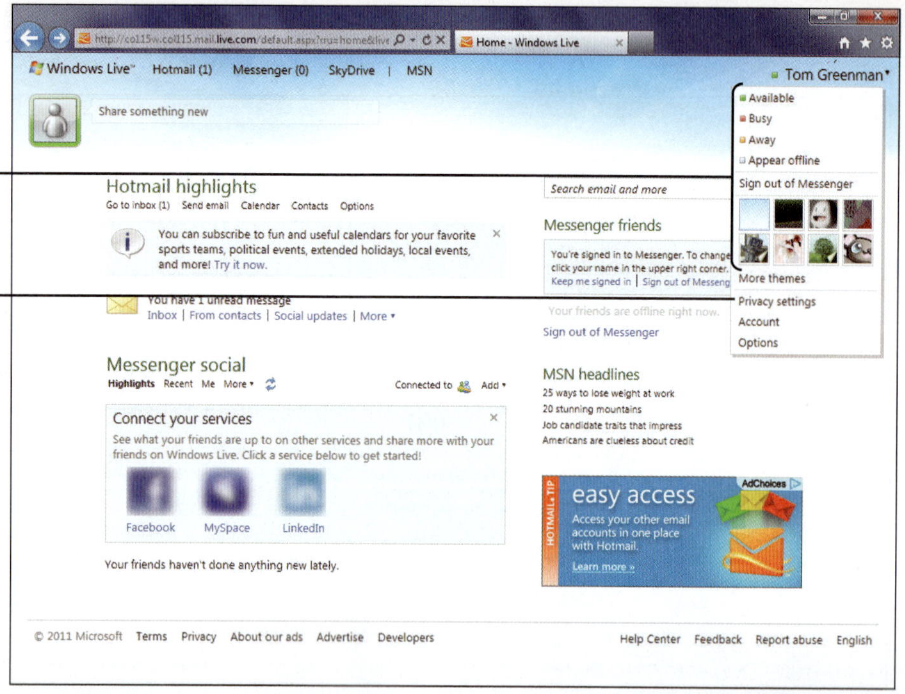

Figure 1

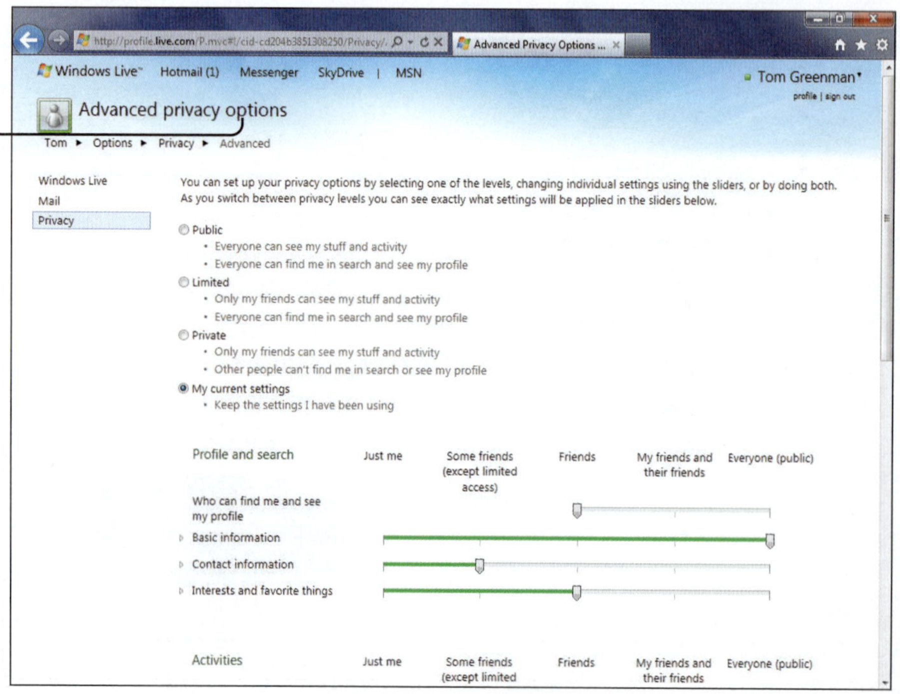

Figure 2

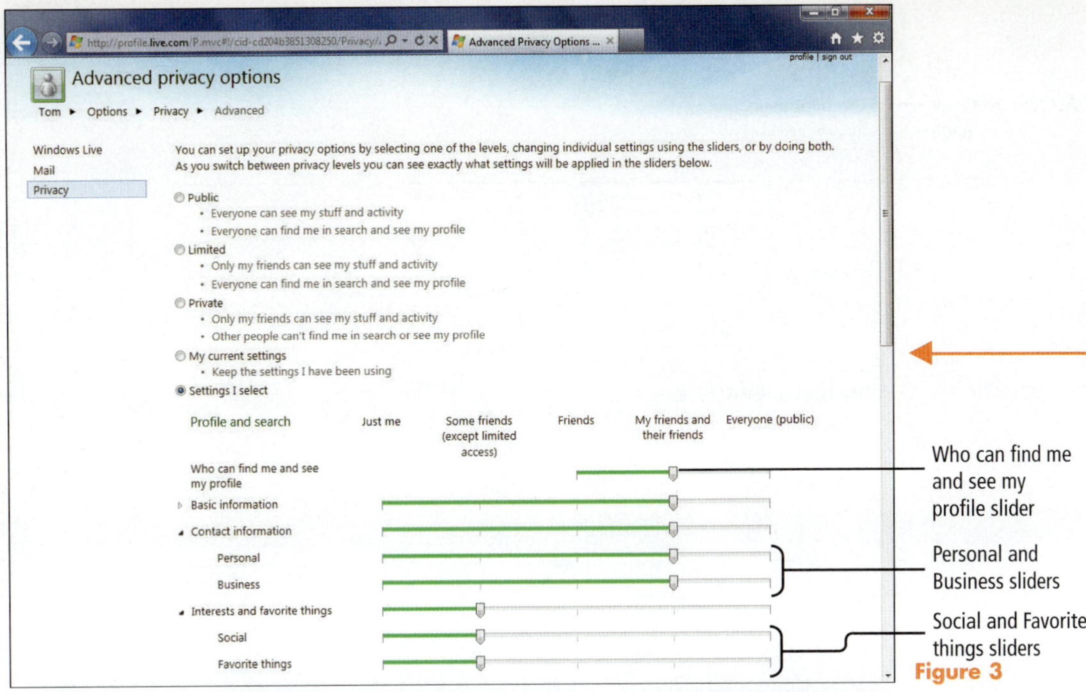

Figure 3

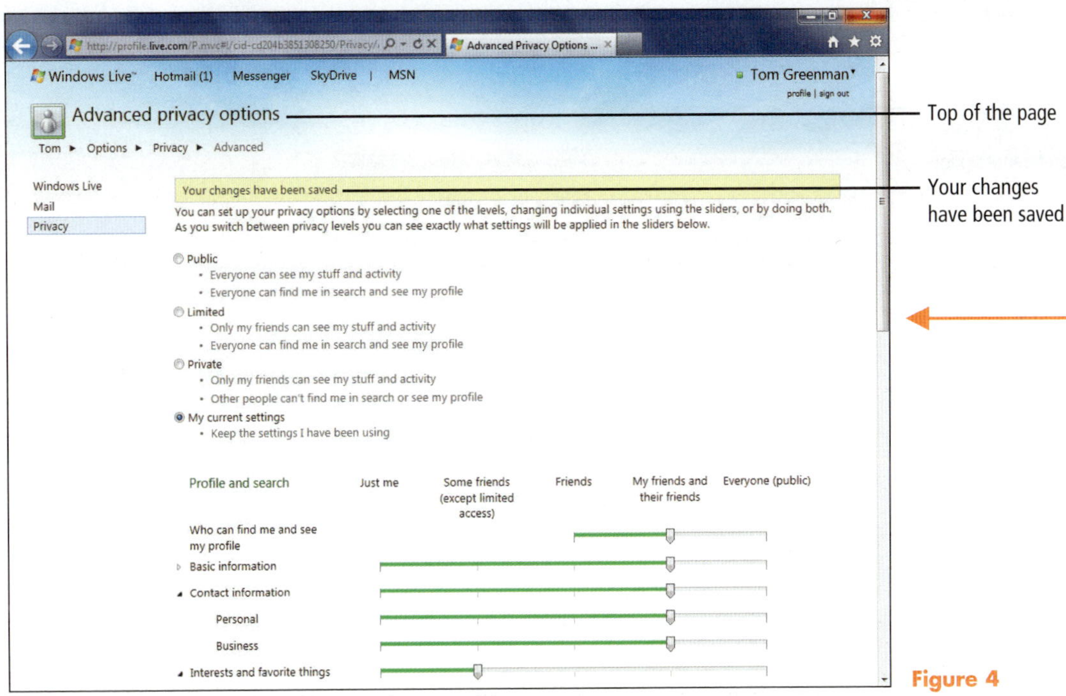

Figure 4

6. If necessary, scroll to locate and then click **Interests and favorite things** to display its options. Drag the **Interests and favorite things** slider to **Some friends (except limited access)**, and then compare your screen with **Figure 3**.

   You can change multiple sliders at the same time by dragging its parent slider. Here, three settings were changed at the same time.

7. Scroll to the bottom of the page to the **Who can contact me** section and drag the **Friend and group invitations** slider to **My friends and their friends**. Drag the **Comments** slider to **Some friends (except limited access)**.
8. Click the **Save** button. If necessary, scroll to the top of the page and then compare your screen with **Figure 4**.
9. Click **Start**, click **All Programs**, and then click the **Accessories** folder. Click **Snipping Tool**, click the **New button arrow**, and then click **Full-screen Snip**.
10. Click the **Save Snip** button. In the **Save As** dialog box, navigate to your storage device. Click **New folder**, type Web Apps Chapter 1 and then press Enter two times to accept the name and open the new folder.
11. In the **File name** box, type Lastname_Firstname_wa01_Park_1 Verify that the **Save as type** box displays **JPEG file (*.JPG)**. Then click **Save**. **Close** the **Snipping Tool** window.

■ **You have completed Skill 2 of 10**

- The Account settings enable you to control your marketing preferences and determine whether you receive promotional offers.
- When you add a picture to your Windows Live profile, it will display on your Windows Live page; those you share your profile with will also be able see your picture.

1. In the upper right corner, point to the **Windows Live ID arrow**, and then click **Account**. If necessary, in the **Retype your password** box, type your password, and then click the **Sign in** button. Compare your screen with **Figure 1**.
2. Scroll down, if necessary, to display the **Other options** section, and then click the **Marketing preferences** link.
3. On the **Choose your marketing preferences** page, select each of the three check boxes, and then compare your screen with **Figure 2**.

   These settings enable you to control whether you receive promotional offers from Windows Live, Bing, or MSN. The offers may come to your email address, to your billing address, or phone number.

■ **Continue to the next page to complete the skill**

Account overview page

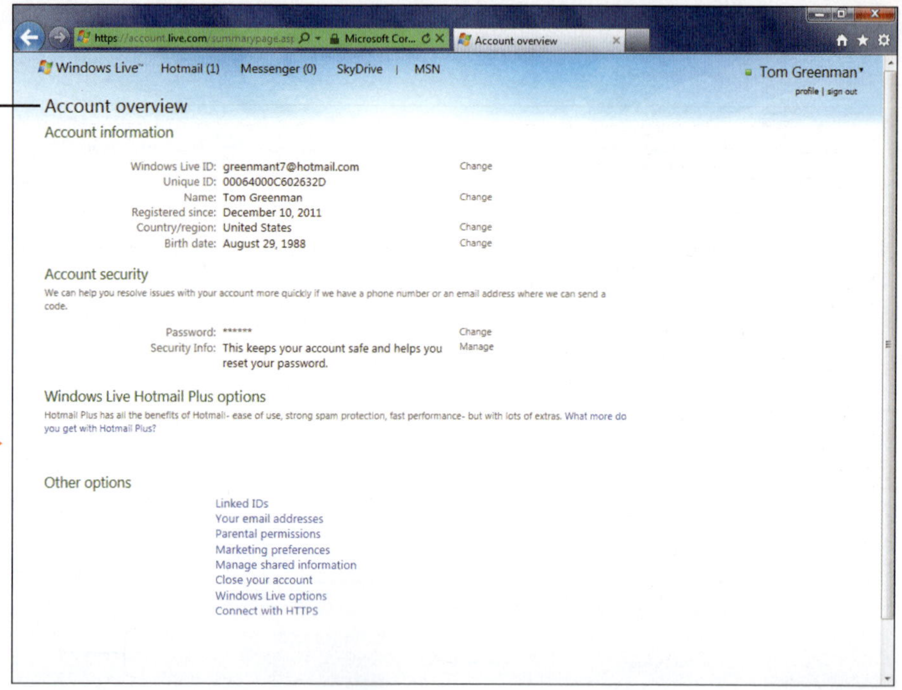

Figure 1

Choose your marketing preferences page

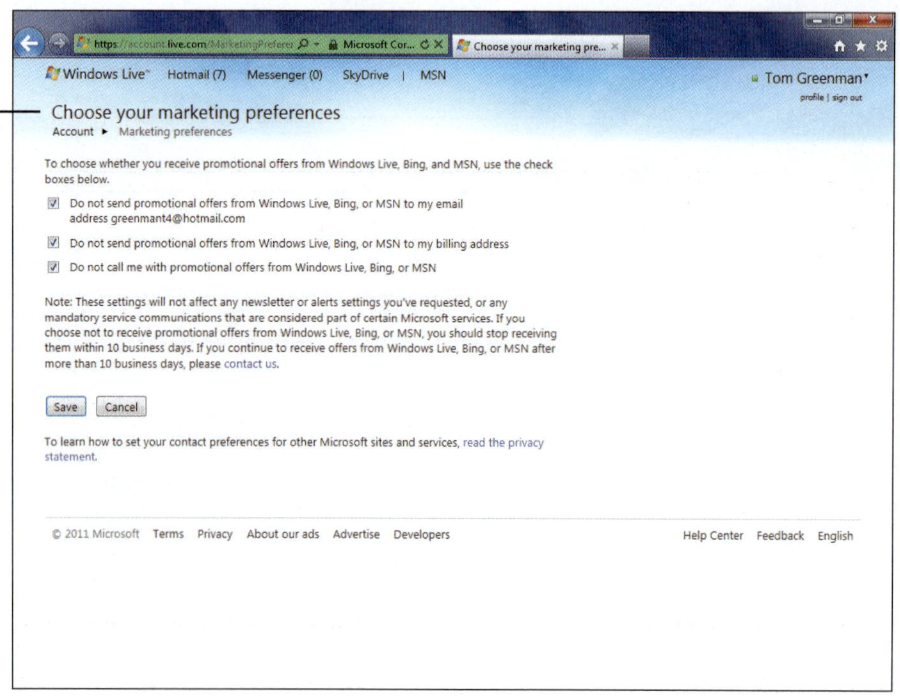

Figure 2

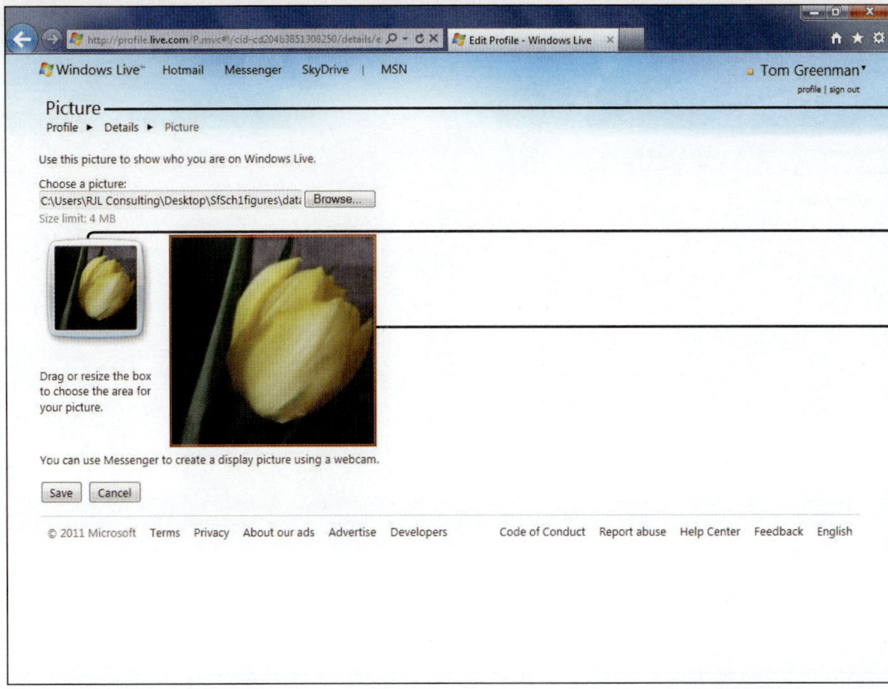

Picture page

How your picture will display (yours may vary)

Drag or resize this box as needed (yours may vary)

Figure 3

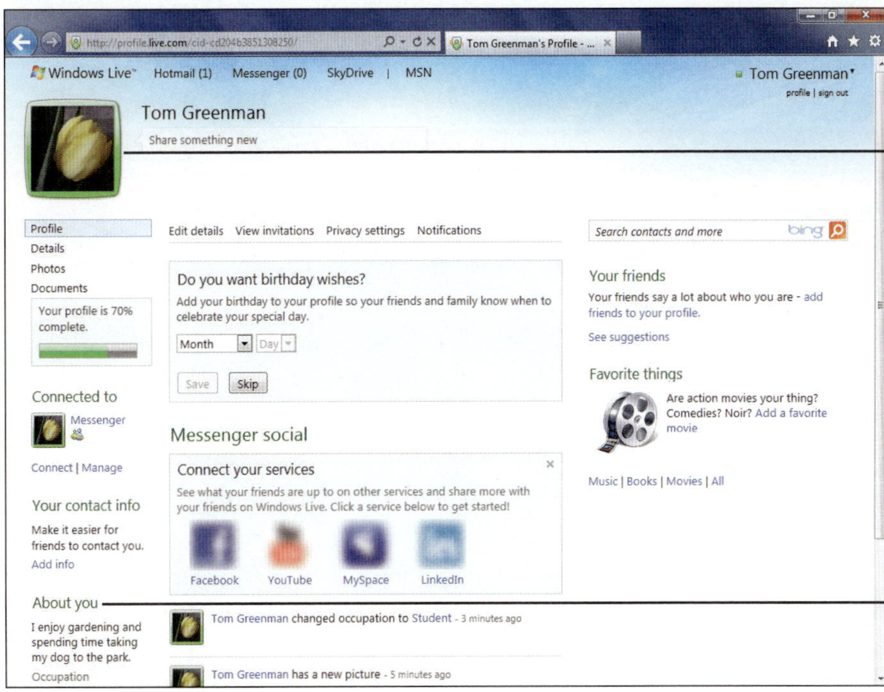

Profile picture (yours may vary)

About you section (yours may vary)

Figure 4

4. On the **Choose your marketing preferences** page, click the **Save** button.
5. Point to your **Windows Live ID**, and then click **Options**. On the **Options** page, under **Profile**, click the **Picture** link.
6. To the right of the **Choose a picture** box, click the **Browse** button. Navigate to where you have stored your student data files, click **wa01_Park_Profile**, and then click the **Open** button. Alternatively, navigate to and open a picture of yourself.
7. If necessary, drag or resize the selection box to choose an appropriate area for your picture. Compare your screen with **Figure 3**.

   The left side of the page shows how the picture will display in your profile.
8. On the **Picture** page, click the **Save** button to accept the changes and return to the Options page.
9. Under **Profile**, click the **About you** link. In the **Occupation** box, type Student In the **More about you** box, type I enjoy followed by two or three things that you like to do. As an alternative, you can type the name of your class and your instructor's name, and then click the **Save** button.
10. At the top of the **Options** page, point to **Messenger**, and then click **Profile.** Scroll down the page to display the About you section on the left side of the screen, and then compare your screen to **Figure 4**.

- **You have completed Skill 3 of 10**

- Recall that SkyDrive is used to store files and folders. A ***folder*** is used to organize similar or related files and information.
- In SkyDrive, you can add descriptions to clarify the use or purpose of the files contained inside of your folders.

1. On the navigation bar above your profile picture, click **SkyDrive**. Compare your screen with **Figure 1**.

   SkyDrive is organized into three sections: Files, Documents, and Photos. Files and Documents store all of your files and folders. Photos stores your photos and photo albums.

2. On the SkyDrive navigation bar, click the **New folder** link.
3. In the **New folder** box, type Seasonal Events and then compare your screen with **Figure 2**.
4. Press **Enter** on your keyboard. Then click the folder's name.

■ **Continue to the next page to complete the skill**

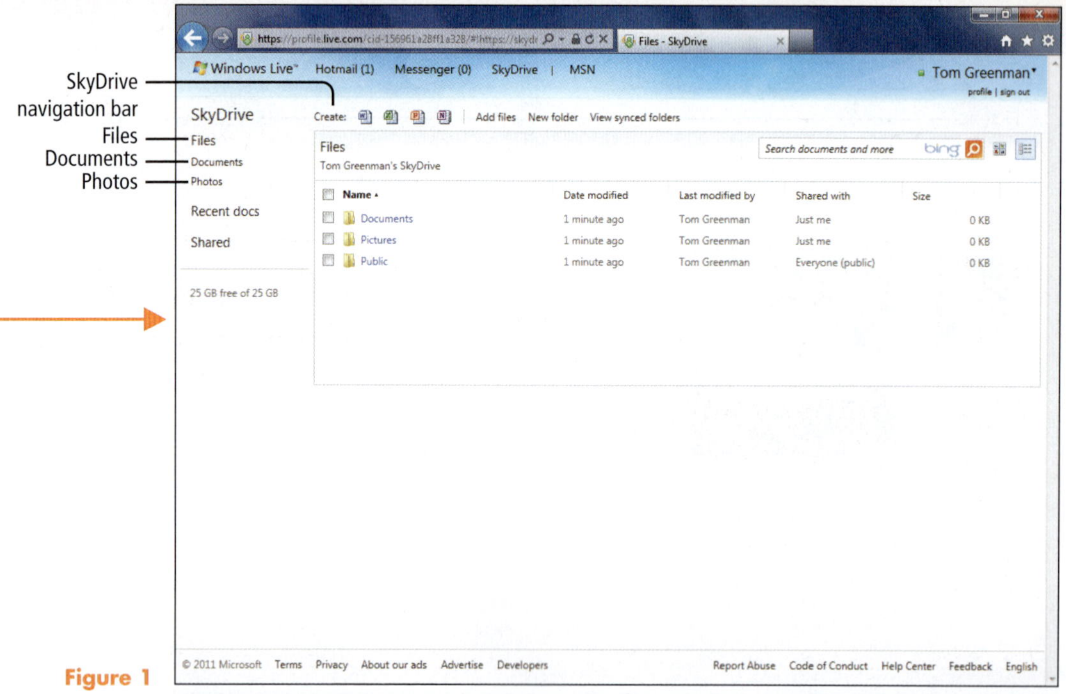

Figure 1

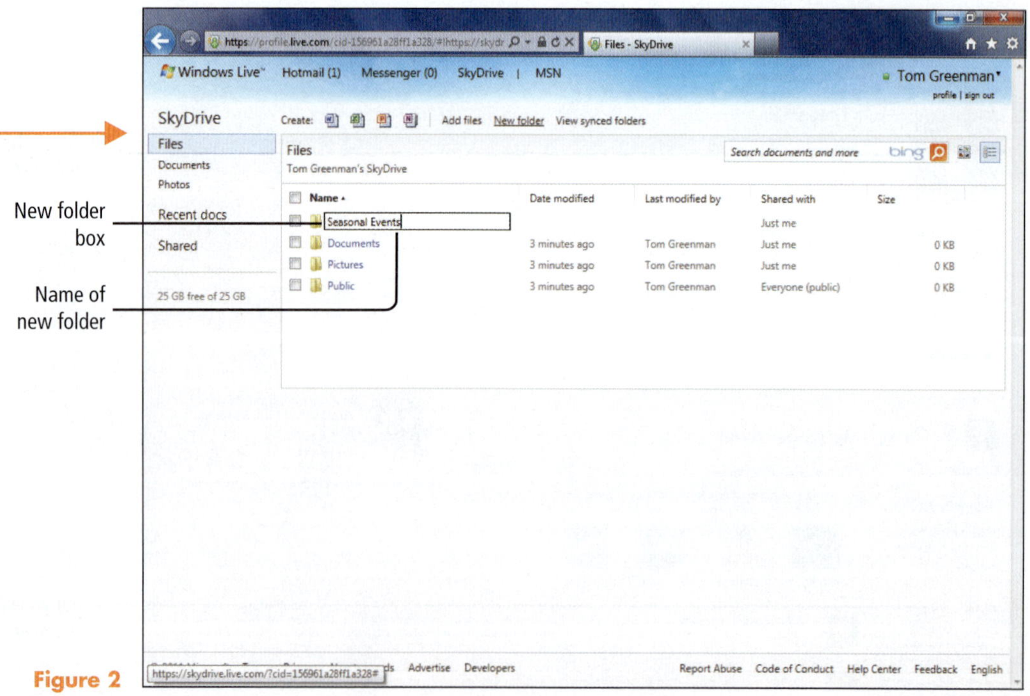

Figure 2

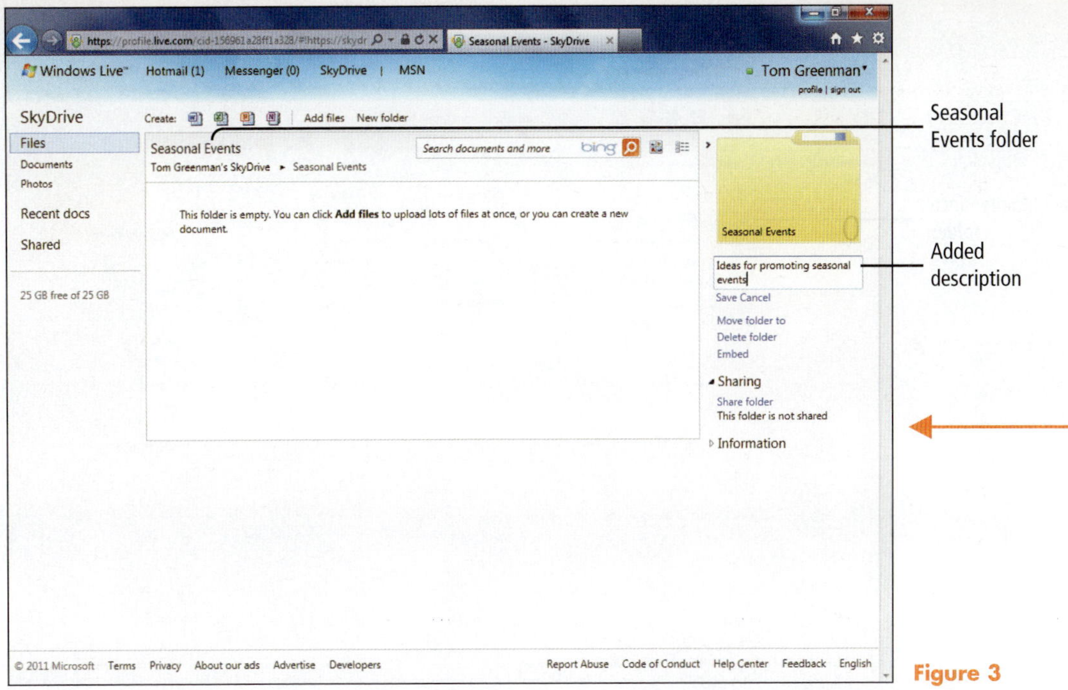

Figure 3

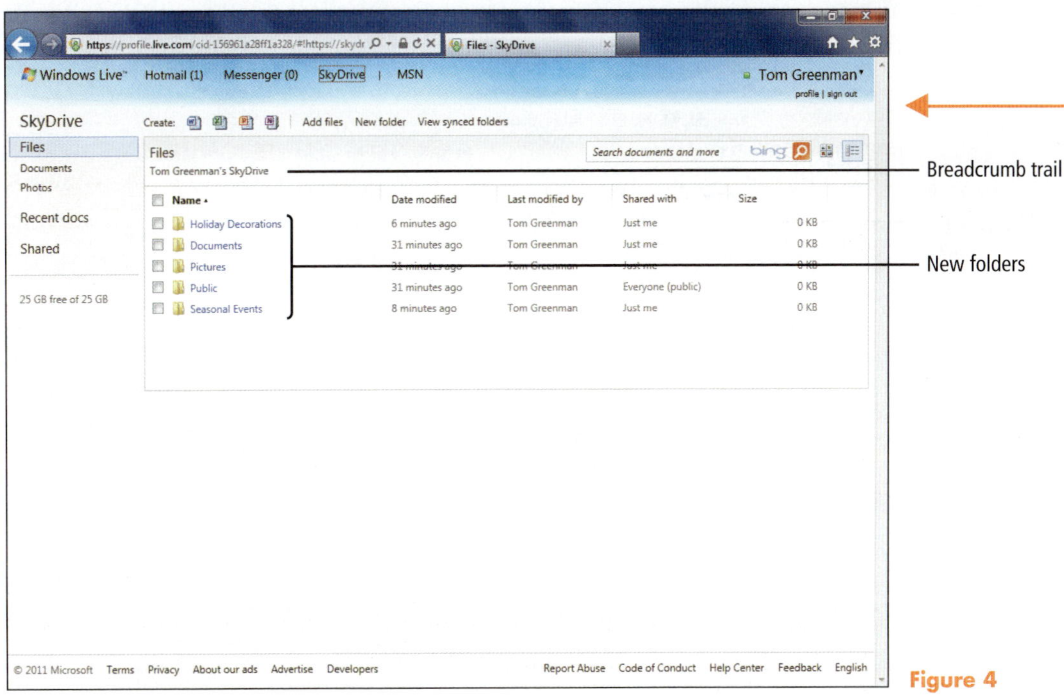

Figure 4

5. In the right pane, below the Seasonal Events folder image, click **Add a description**. Type Ideas for promoting seasonal events Compare your screen with **Figure 3**. Notice the breadcrumb trail and then click Save.

   A ***breadcrumb trail*** is a text navigation bar that shows your place in a hierarchy of web pages or nested folders and files. Here, the breadcrumb trail indicates that SkyDrive is a subfolder of Tom Greenman.

6. In the left pane, click **Files**. On the SkyDrive navigation bar, click **New folder**. In the **New folder** box, type Holiday Decorations Press **Enter** on your keyboard.

7. In the right pane, below the Holiday Decorations folder image, click **Add a description**. Type Holiday Decorations Inventory by Park and then click **Save**.

8. In the breadcrumb trail, click **SkyDrive**. Compare your screen with **Figure 4**.

■ **You have completed Skill 4 of 10**

- In SkyDrive, you can add a ***subfolder***, which is a folder inside another folder.
- After subfolders are created, you can organize folders and subfolders by moving them around and renaming them.

1. On the SkyDrive navigation bar, click the **New folder** link. In the **New folder** box, type Park Maintenance and then press **Enter**. Compare your screen with **Figure 1**.
2. Click the Park Maintenance folder, and then click the **New folder** link. Type Fall Maintenance Press **Enter** to create the new subfolder and then compare your screen with **Figure 2**.
3. While still in **Park Maintenance**, click the **New folder** link and type Spring Maintenance Press **Enter** to create a second new subfolder.
4. Click the **New folder** link and type December Events Press **Enter** to create a third new subfolder.

■ **Continue to the next page to complete the skill**

Park Maintenance folder

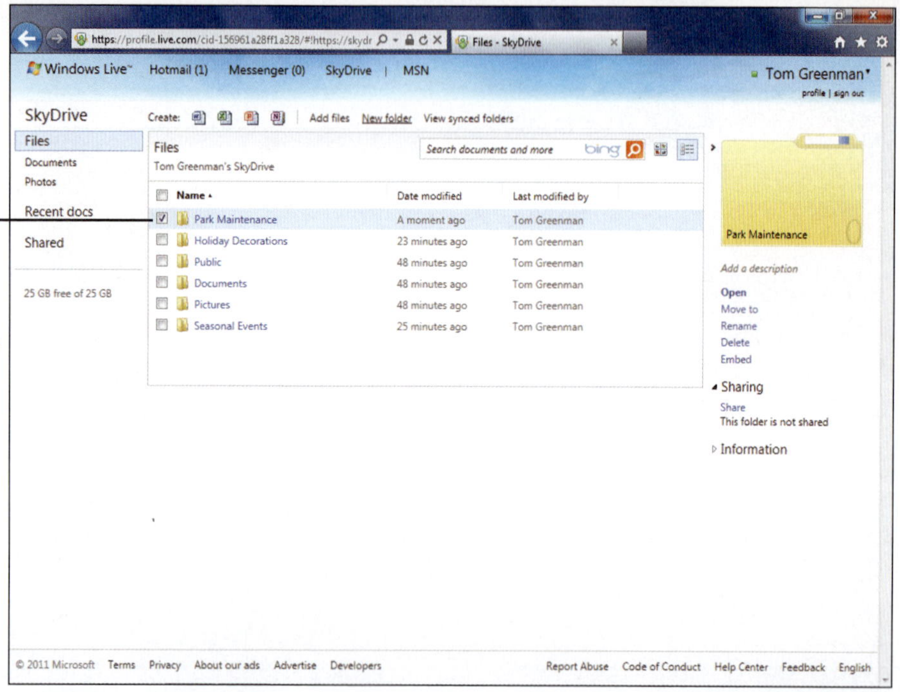

Figure 1

New Fall Maintenance folder

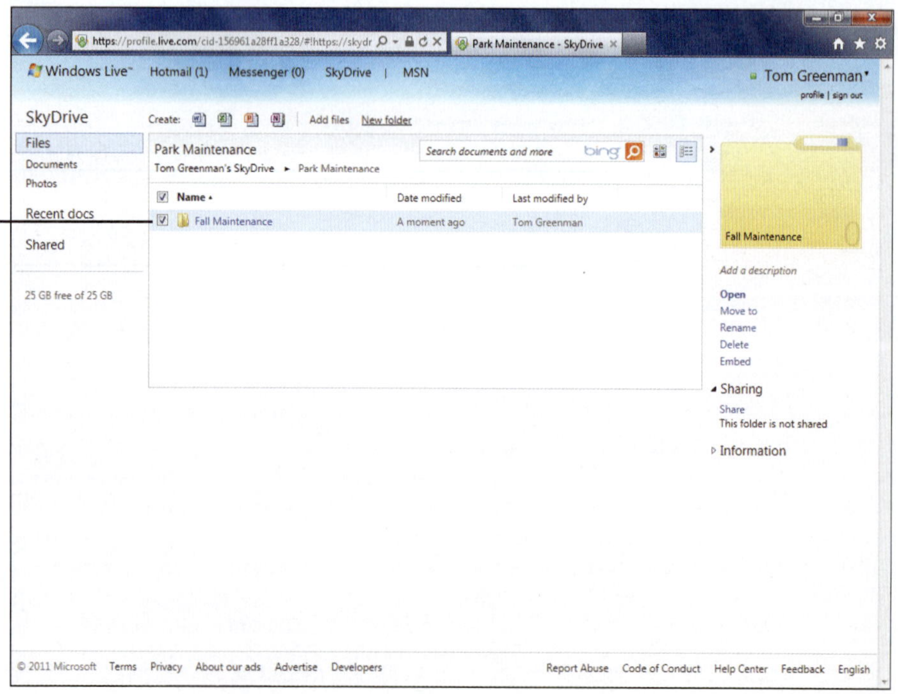

Figure 2

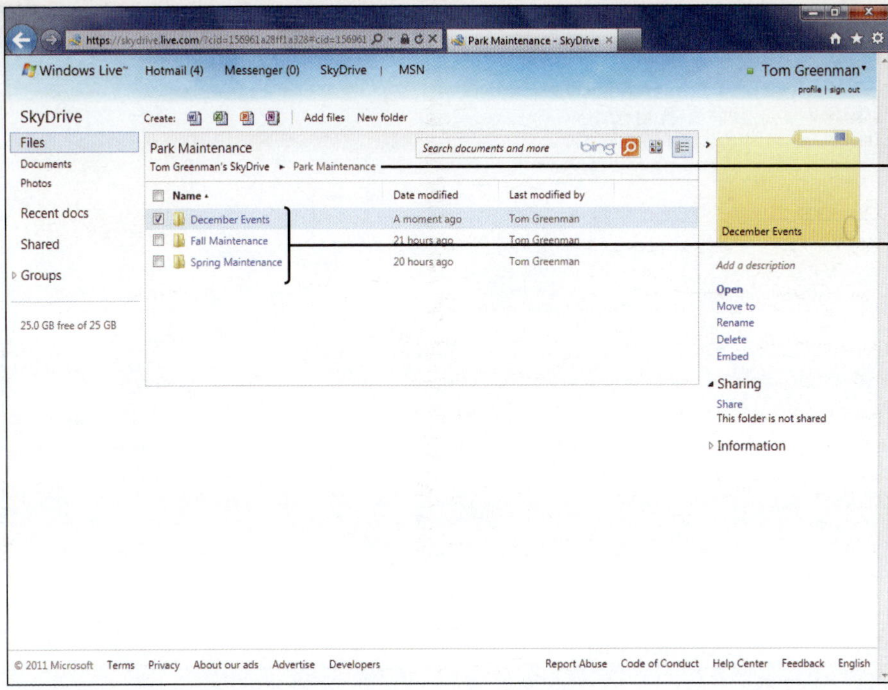

Figure 3

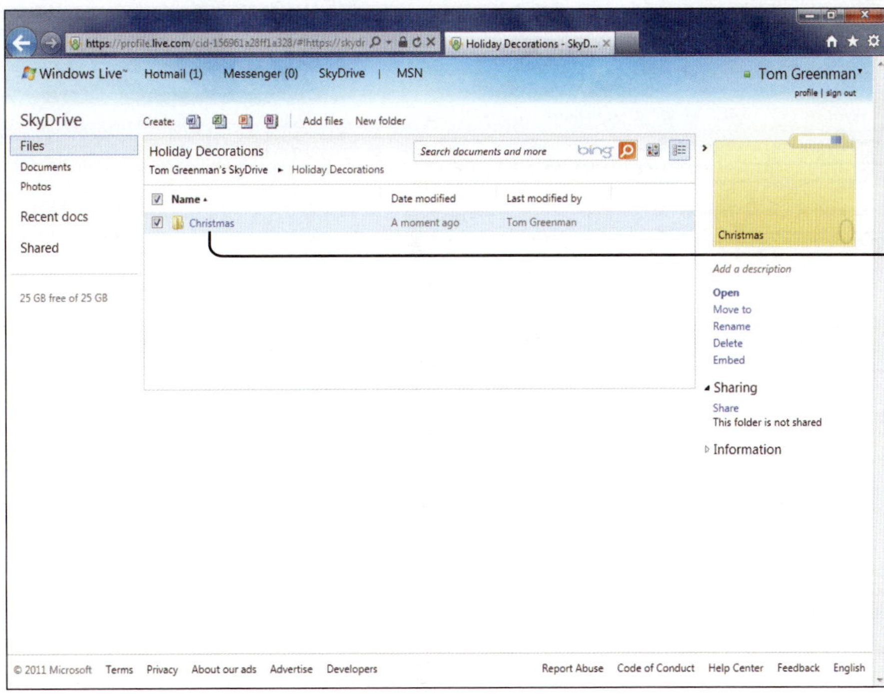

Figure 4

5. Notice the breadcrumb trail, and then compare your screen with **Figure 3**.

   There are now three subfolders inside the Park Maintenance folder.

6. Uncheck Fall Maintenance and then check the **December Events** folder, and then in the right pane, click **Move to.**
7. On the **The selected item will be moved to: box**, click **Holiday Decorations.** Click **Move**.
8. On the breadcrumb trail, click **Tom Greenmans' SkyDrive**. Click the **Holiday Decorations** folder.
9. Click the **December Events** check box and then click **Rename**. In the **New name** box, replace the text with Christmas and then press **Enter**. Compare your screen with **Figure 4**.
10. Click **Start**, click **All Programs**, and then click the **Accessories** folder. Click **Snipping Tool**, click the **New button arrow**, and then click **Full-screen Snip**.
11. Click the **Save Snip** button. In the **Save As** dialog box, navigate to your storage device. Open the **Web Apps Chapter 1** folder.
12. In the **File name** box, type Lastname_Firstname_wa01_Park_2 Verify that the **Save as type** box displays **JPEG file (*.JPG)**. Then click **Save**. **Close** the **Snipping Tool** window.
13. At the top of the page, click **SkyDrive.**

■ **You have completed Skill 5 of 10**

- You can upload files that are stored on your computer to your SkyDrive folders.
- After you upload files, you can then rename and move the files around within your SkyDrive folders.

1. Near the middle of the SkyDrive page, click **Documents folder**.
2. In the SkyDrive navigation bar, click the **New folder** link. In the **Name** box, type Accounts Payable and then press **Enter**. Compare your screen with **Figure 1**.

   The Accounts Payable folder is a subfolder of the Documents folder.
3. Click **Accounts Payable**. On the SkyDrive navigation bar, click **Add files**. Click **select them from your computer**. Navigate to where you have stored your student data files, click **wa01_Park_Statement**, and then click the **Open** button. Compare your screen with **Figure 2**.
4. Click the **wa01_Park_Statement** check box. In the right pane, click **Rename**. In the **New name** box, replace the text with May Statement and then press **Enter**.
5. On the breadcrumb trail, click **your SkyDrive**. Click the **Park Maintenance** folder to open it, and then click the **Spring Maintenance** folder.

   The Spring Maintenance folder is a subfolder of the Park Maintenance folder.

■ **Continue to the next page to complete the skill**

Accounts Payable is a subfolder of Documents

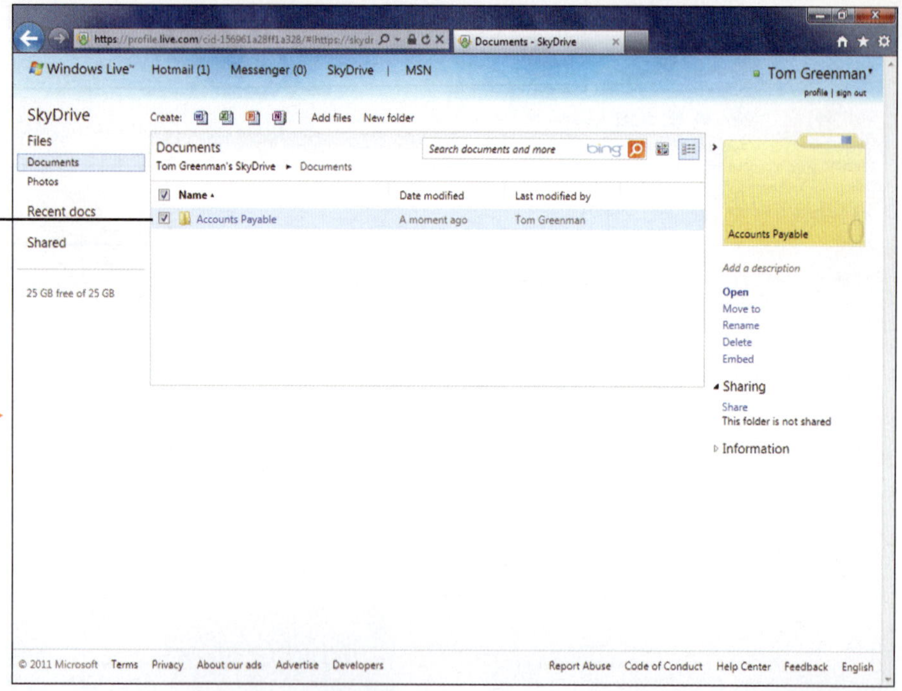

Figure 1

Breadcrumb trail

Uploaded file

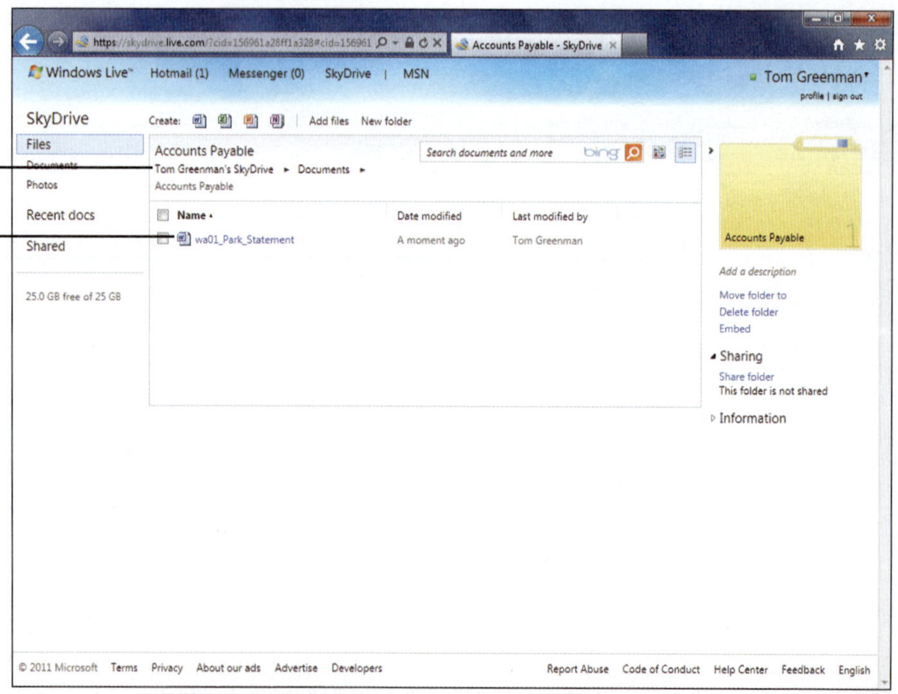

Figure 2

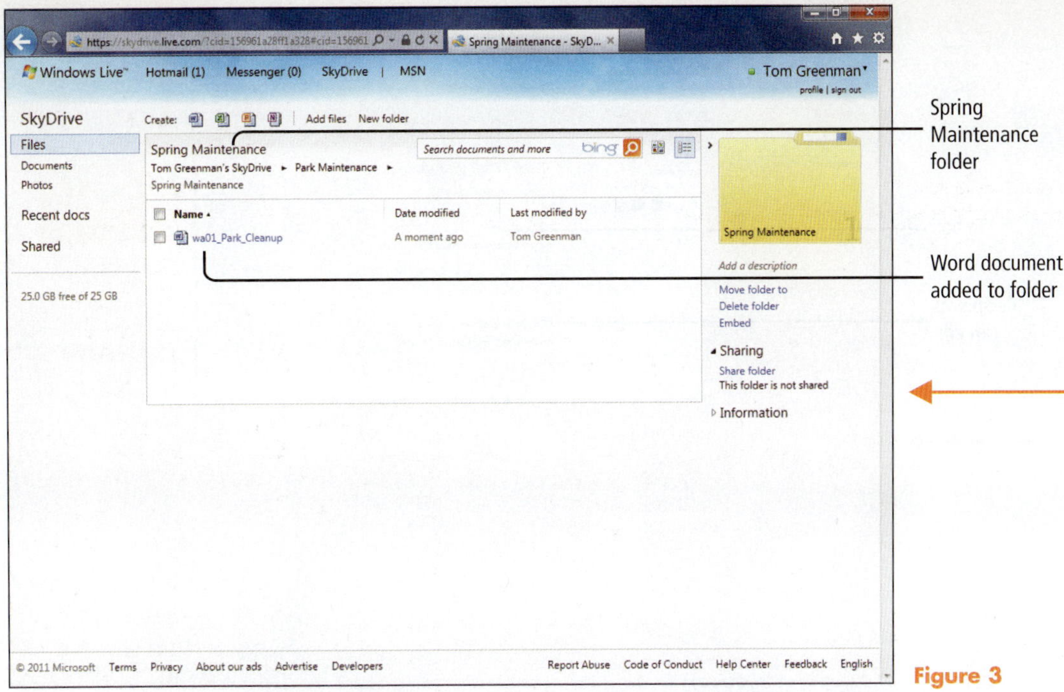

Figure 3

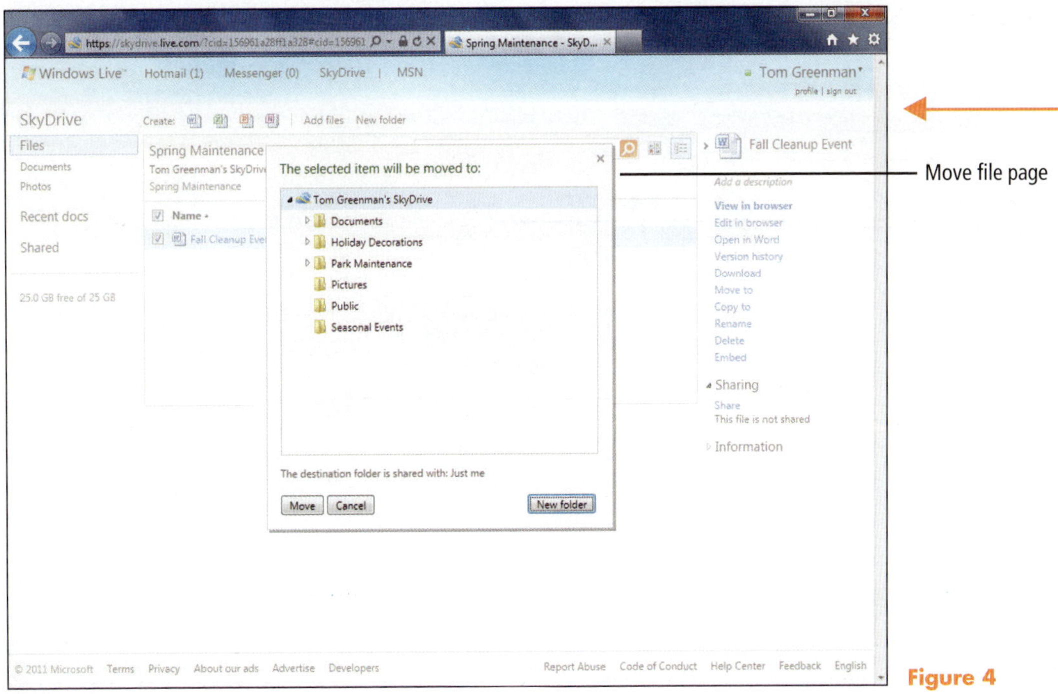

Figure 4

6. On the SkyDrive navigation bar, click **Add files**. Click **select them from your computer**. Navigate to where you have stored your student data files. Click **wa01_Park_Cleanup**, and then click the **Open** button. After the file uploads, compare your screen with **Figure 3**.
7. Click the **wa01_Park_Cleanup** check box, and then click **Rename**. In the **New Name** box, type Fall Cleanup Event and then press **Enter**.
8. In the right pane, click **Move to**. Compare your screen with **Figure 4**.
9. Click **Seasonal Events**, and then click **Move**.
10. Click **Start**, click **All Programs**, and then click the **Accessories** folder. Click **Snipping Tool**, click the **New button arrow**, and then click **Full-screen Snip**.
11. Click the **Save Snip** button. In the **Save As** dialog box, navigate to your storage device. Open the **Web Apps Chapter 1** folder.
12. In the **File name** box, type Lastname_Firstname_wa01_Park_3 Verify that the **Save as type** box displays **JPEG file (*.JPG)**. Then click **Save**. **Close** the **Snipping Tool** window.
13. At the top of the page, click **SkyDrive**.

■ **You have completed Skill 6 of 10**

- ***Permissions*** are settings that allow another person to access, read, modify, or delete files or folders.
- By default, the Documents folder, and the files within that folder, are personal and are not shared with others.

1. In the SkyDrive navigation bar, click **New folder**. In the **New folder** box, type Park Planning press **Enter**.
2. In the right pane, click **Share**. Compare your screen with **Figure 1**.
3. In the **To:** box, type your instructor's email address.
4. Include the following brief message: Here is the Park Planning folder. Compare your screen with **Figure 2**.

■ **Continue to the next page to complete the skill**

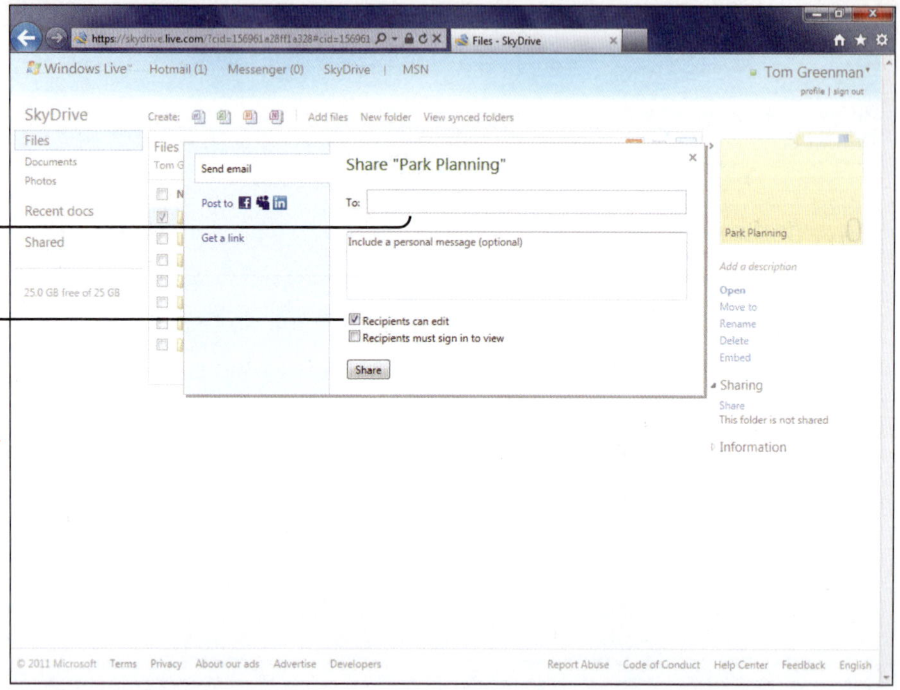

Figure 1

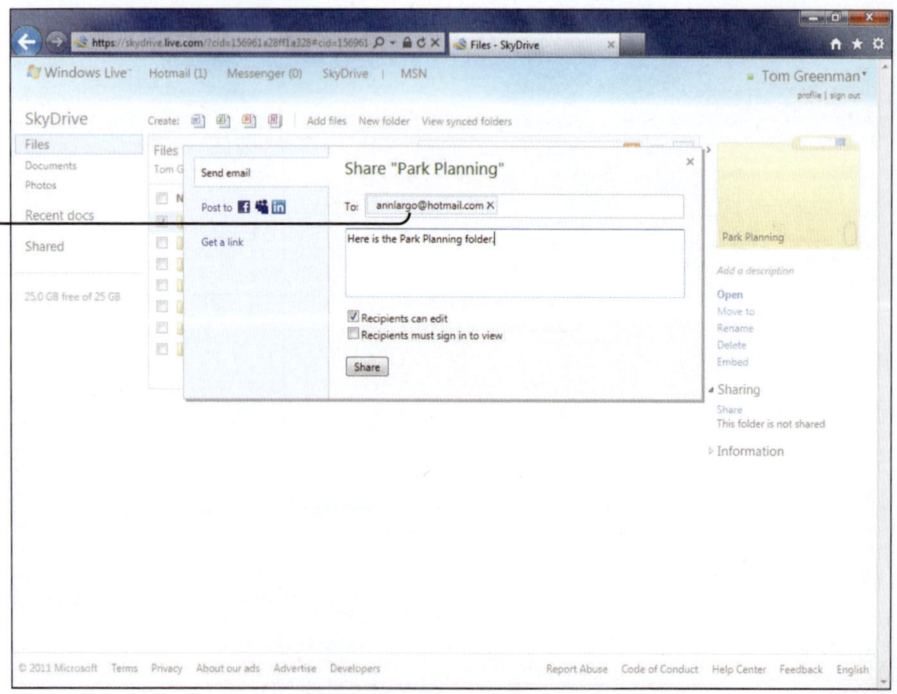

Figure 2

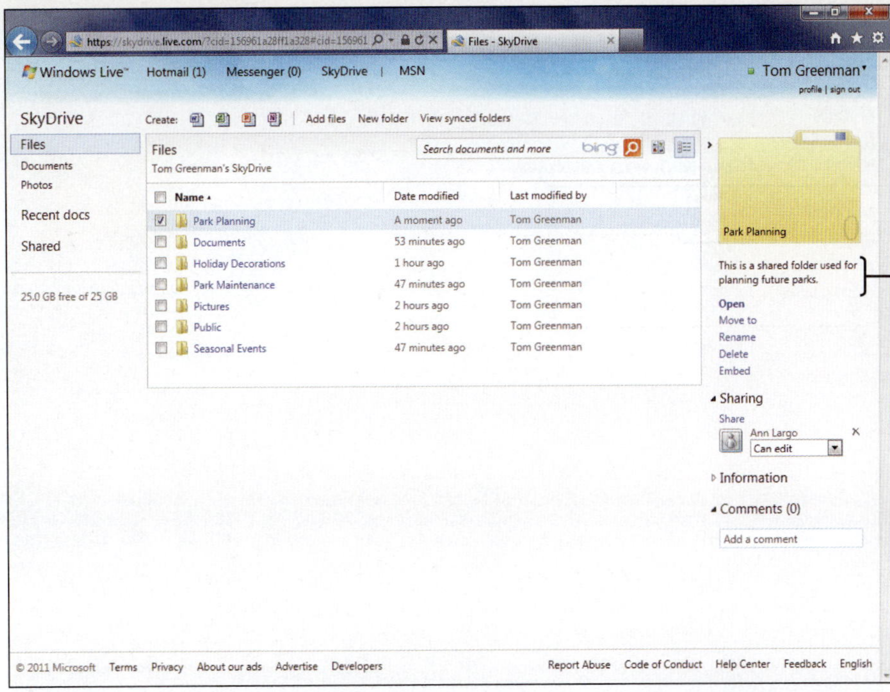

Figure 3

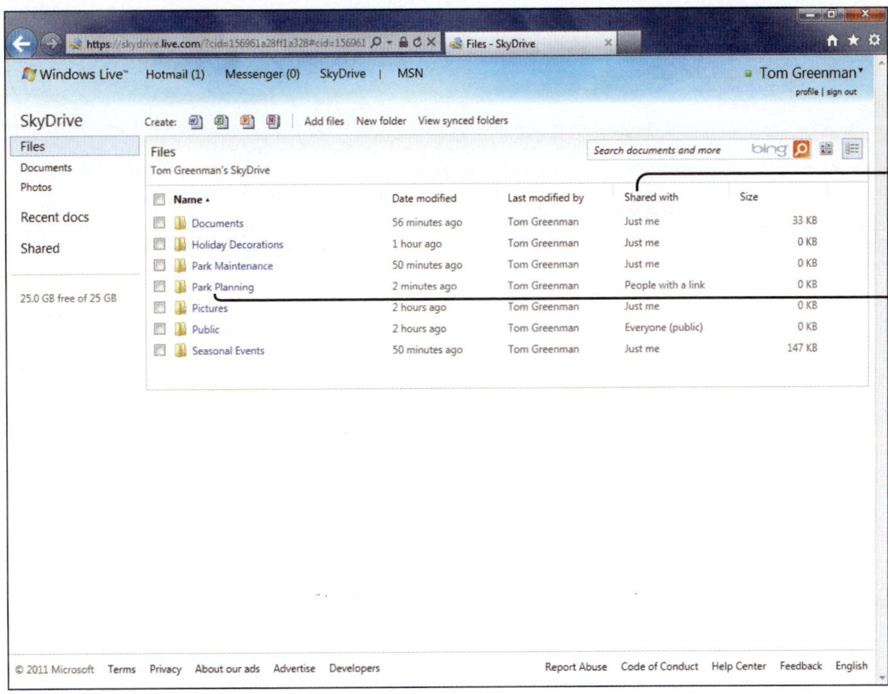

Figure 4

5. Select the **Recipients must sign in to view Windows Live ID** check box, and then click the **Share** button.
6. If prompted, click the **Please complete this security check** link. Type the CAPTCHA and then click **Continue**.
7. After solving the puzzle, close that tab to return to your SkyDrive. Click **Share** again.
8. In the right pane, click **Add a description** and type This is a shared folder used for planning future parks. Click **Save**, and then compare your screen with **Figure 3**.
9. In the breadcrumb trail, click **SkyDrive**, and then compare your screen with **Figure 4**.

   The Shared with column indicates the sharing status. The Park Planning folder status indicates the folder is shared.

10. Click **Start**, click **All Programs**, and then click the **Accessories** folder. Click **Snipping Tool**, click the **New button arrow**, and then click **Full-screen Snip**.
11. Click the **Save Snip** button. In the **Save As** dialog box, navigate to your storage device. Open the **Web Apps Chapter 1** folder.
12. In the **File name** box, type Lastname_Firstname_wa01_Park_4 Verify that the **Save as type** box displays **JPEG file (*.JPG)**. Then click **Save**. **Close** the **Snipping Tool** window.

- **You have completed Skill 7 of 10**

- You can share folders by sending links to others enabling them to view all the files in that folder by clicking the link.
- Public links can be shared by email or social networking sites such as Facebook, MySpace, or LinkedIn, or they can be posted on a website.

---

1. In the SkyDrive navigation bar, click **New folder**. In the **New folder** box, type Public Park Events press **Enter**.
2. Click the folder, and then click **Add** files. Click the **Public Park Events** folders and then click **Add** files. the **select them from your computer** link. Navigate to where you have stored your student data files. Click **wa01_Park_Rally**, and then click the **Open** button. Compare your screen with **Figure 1**.
3. Click the check box next to **wa01_Park_ Rally**. Click **Rename**, type Community Pep Rally and then press **Enter**.
4. In the breadcrumb trail, click **your SkyDrive**. Click **Public Park Events**. In the right pane, under **Sharing**, click **Share folder**. Click **Get a link** and then in the **Make it public!** section, click **Get a link** button. Compare your screen with **Figure 2**.

   The public link can be used to allow anyone with a link to the folder to see what you're sharing.

■ Continue to the next page to complete the skill

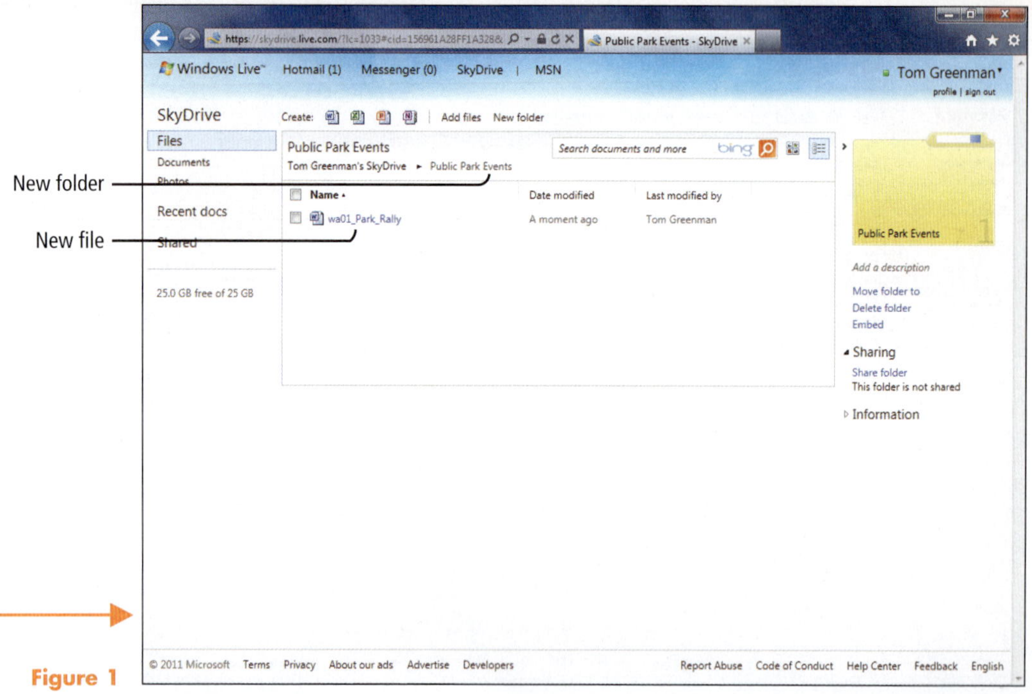

Figure 1

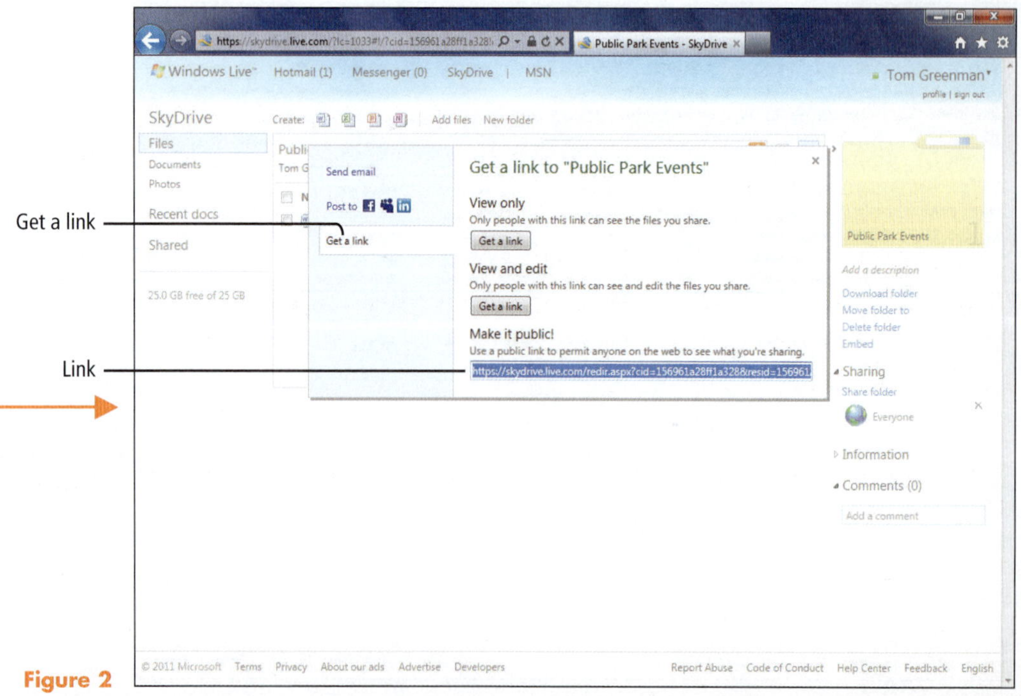

Figure 2

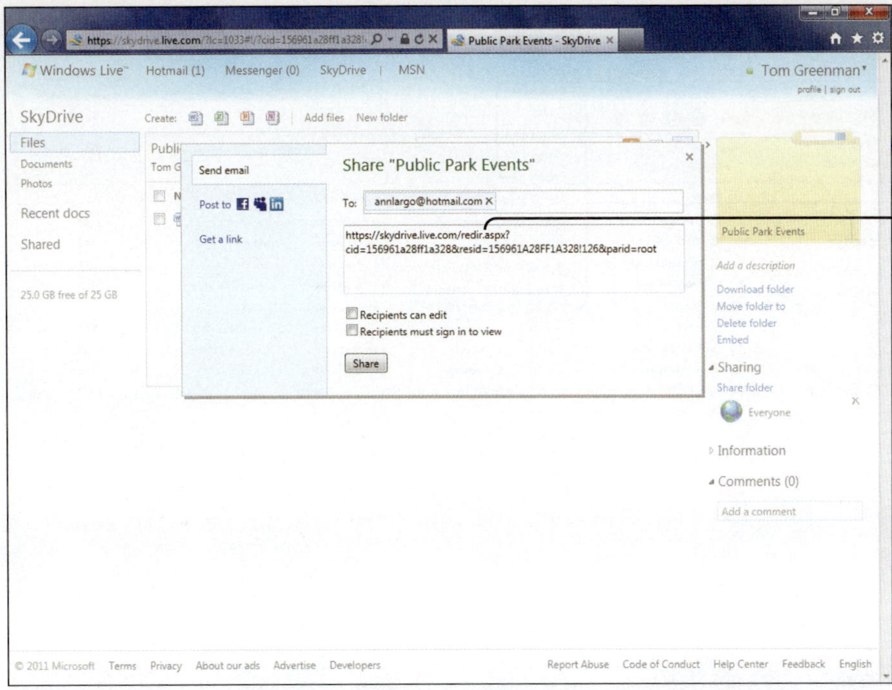

Figure 3

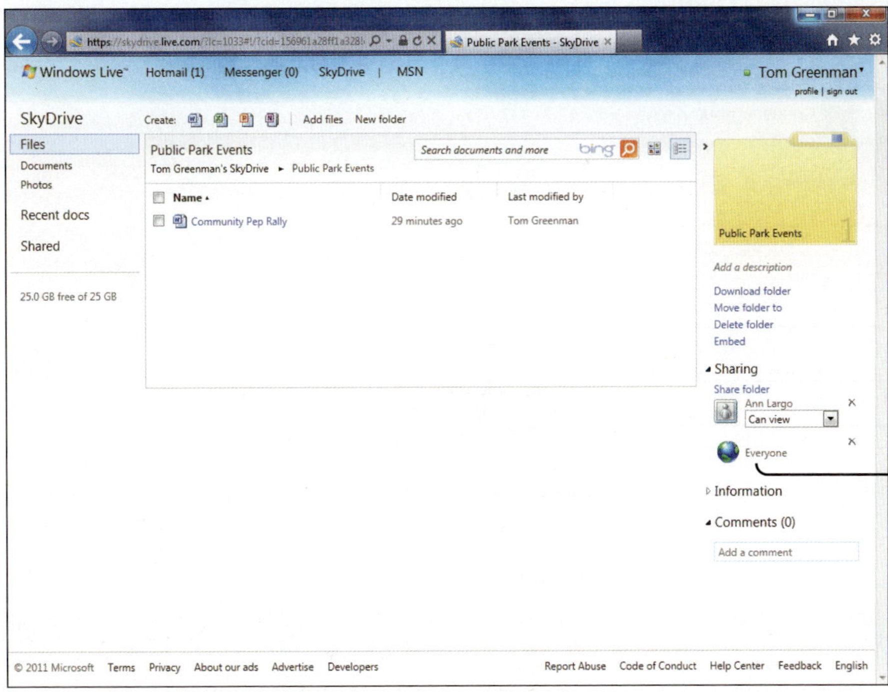

Figure 4

5. Right-click the highlighted link and then click **Copy**. In the left pane, click **Send** email.

   The Get a link option enables you to copy the link and then paste it into a social networking site or an email message. The Send email option enables you to enter an email address so that a link to the folder can be sent.

6. In the **To** box, type your instructor's email address. In the personal message box, right-click and then click **Paste**. Click once in the **Recipient can edit** check box. Compare your screen with **Figure 3**.

   Anyone who receives an email with a link to a public folder will be able to access the files in that folder without being signed in to Windows Live. For this reason, a folder with the Everyone permission setting should only store files that you are willing to share with anyone.

7. Click the Share button. Compare your screen with **Figure 4**.

   The Sharing section shows that the Public Park Events folder is shared with your instructor and with Everyone.

- **You have completed Skill 8 of 10**

- ▶ Windows Live groups can be created to facilitate communication and collaboration between members.
- ▶ When you create a group, a group website and group email address are also created.

1. At the top of the page, point to **SkyDrive**, and then compare your screen with **Figure 1**.
2. From the **SkyDrive menu**, click **Groups**. On the **Groups** page, click the **Create a group** button.
3. On the **Create a group** page, in the **Name your group** box, type Lastname_ Firstname_AFParks Click the **Check availability** link, and then compare your screen with **Figure 2**.

   Two Windows Live groups cannot have the same name. For this reason, you may need to try more than one name to find one that is available.

4. If your instructor provided an email address or list of email addresses to use in this project, type them in the **Add People** box with a comma between each address. Otherwise, type the email address of a friend you can trust.

■ **Continue to the next page to complete the skill**

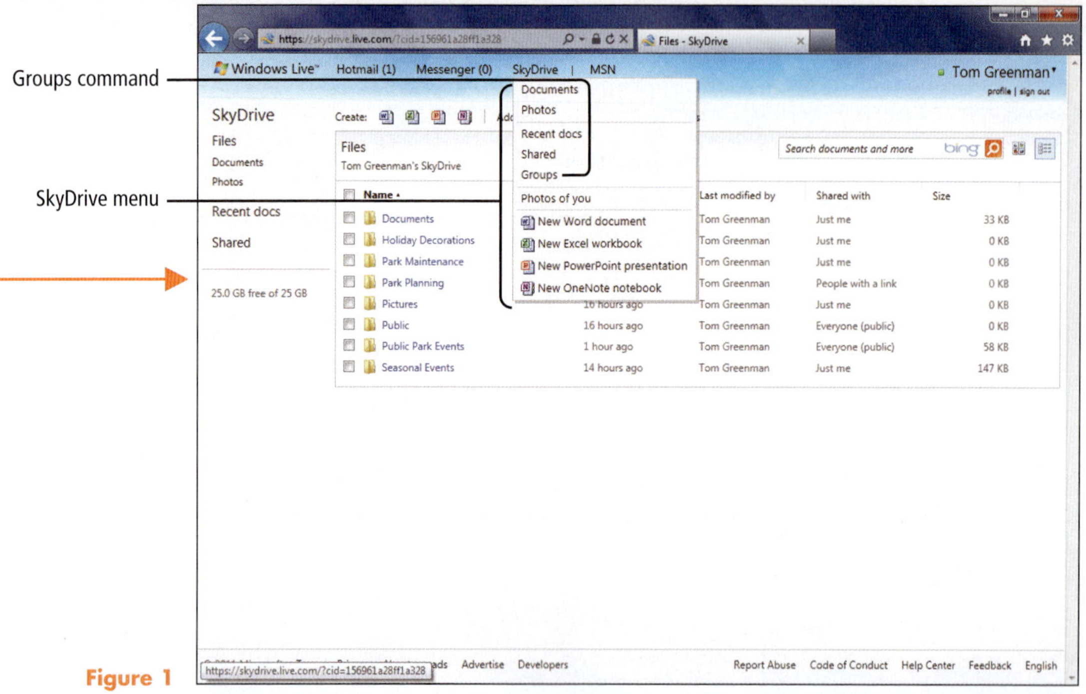

Figure 1

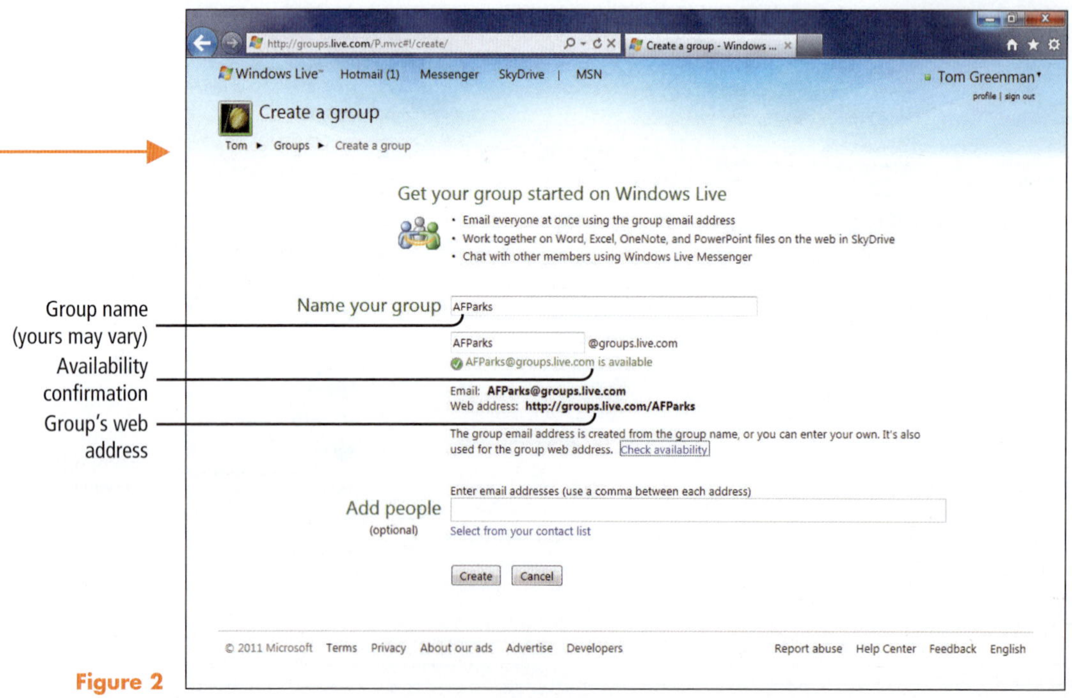

Figure 2

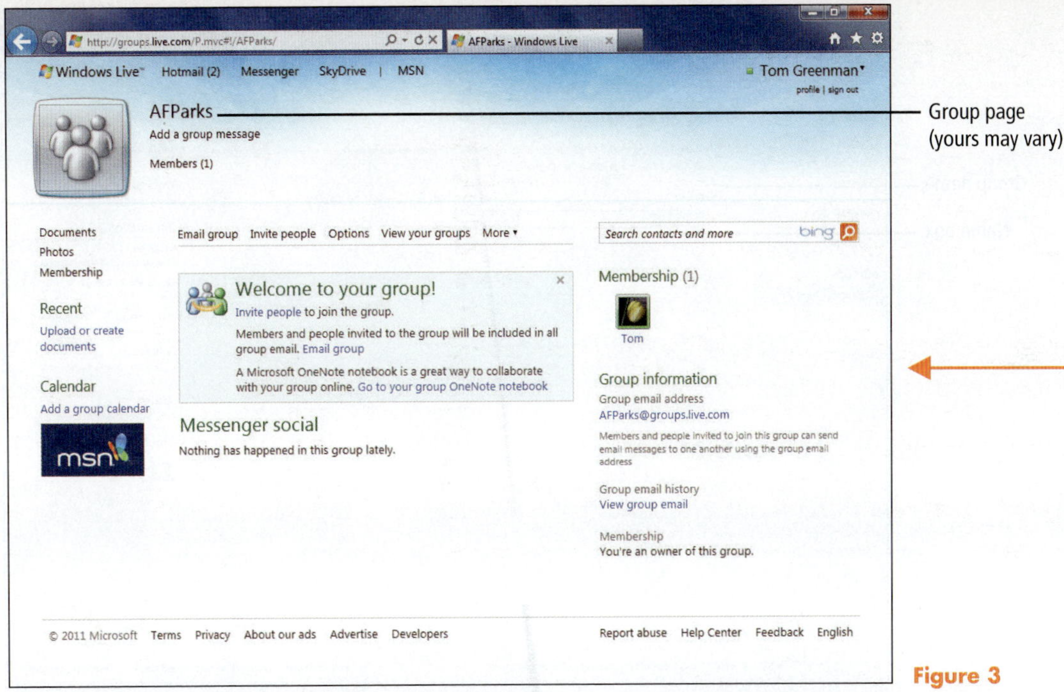

Figure 3

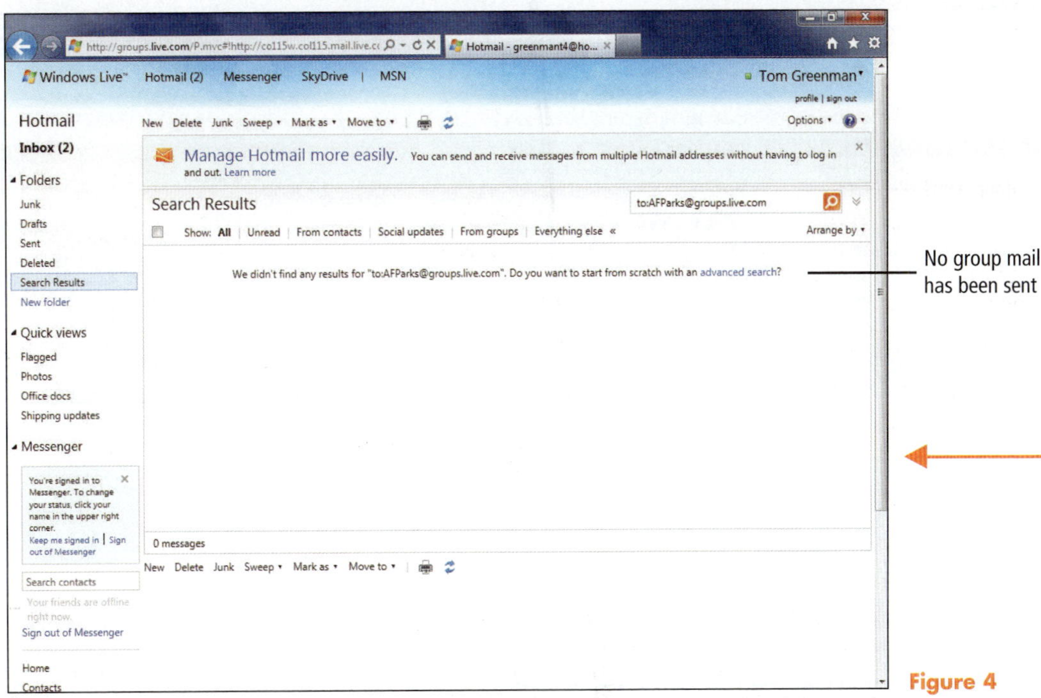

Figure 4

5. Click the **Create** button, and then, if necessary, click **Done**. Compare your screen with **Figure 3**.

   When you add people to a group, invitations are sent to each email address. The email message includes a link that opens the group's page. Each member of the group will need to log on to their Windows Live account before they can view the group's pages or share files.

6. On the left side of your group's home page, click **Membership**.

   The Group membership roles are Owners, Co-Owners, and Members. The person who creates the group is the owner but can invite another person to become the co-owner. Members are those who accept an invitation to join the group.

7. Below **Other**, click **Invites**.

   Members that have not yet accepted invitations are listed here.

8. In the breadcrumb trail, click **your group name** to display your group's home page. In the lower right side of the screen, locate the **Group email history** section, click **View group email**, and then compare your screen with **Figure 4**.

   Email is a primary way to communicate with your group. You will likely not have any email until there are more members in your group and they have used the group's email address to compose and send an email message.

9. At the top of the page, point to **SkyDrive**, and then click **Groups**.

- **You have completed Skill 9 of 10**

▸ SKILL 10: Create Group Folders

▸ You can upload files to your group's SkyDrive and then add a description.

1. If necessary, point to **SkyDrive**, and then click **Groups**.

   Any group that you belong to is listed here. Each group will have its own set of links to view documents, view photos, and to invite others. You can click the group's name to access its links.

2. For the group you just created, click **View documents**. On the SkyDrive navigation bar, click **New folder**. Compare your screen with **Figure 1**.
3. In the **New folder** box, replace the text with Our Suggestion Box Press **Enter**.
4. Under **Sharing**, verify that the **Members can edit option** is selected. Compare your screen with **Figure 2**.

■ **Continue to the next page to complete the skill**

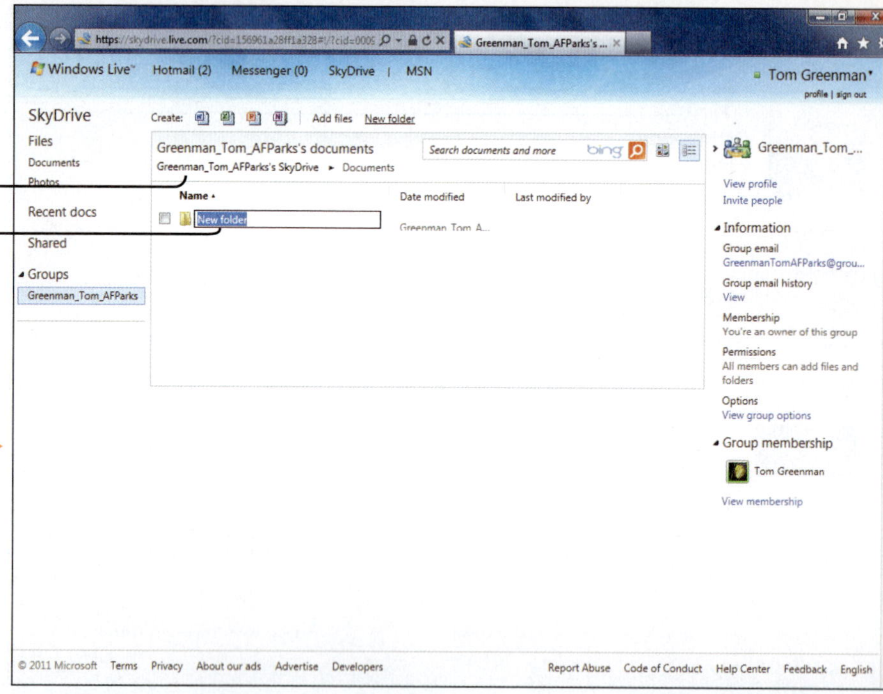

Figure 1

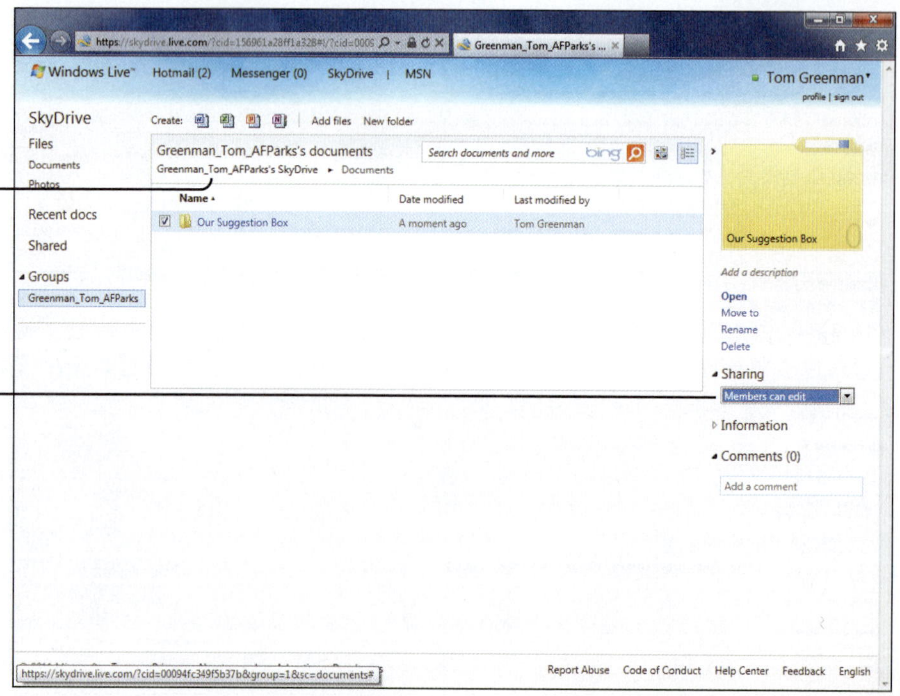

Figure 2

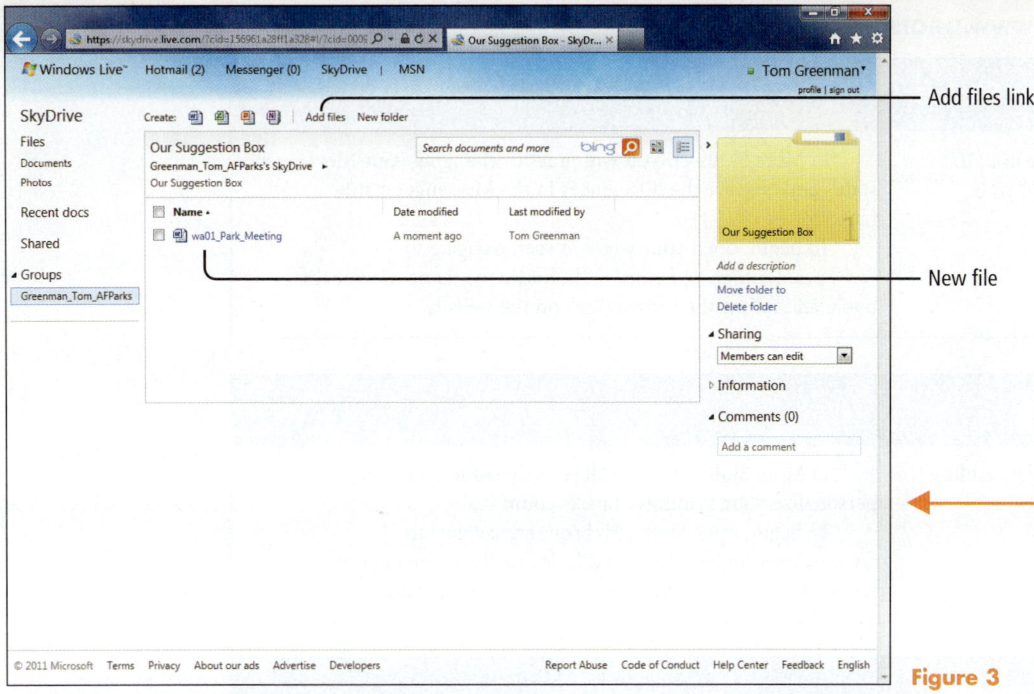

Figure 3

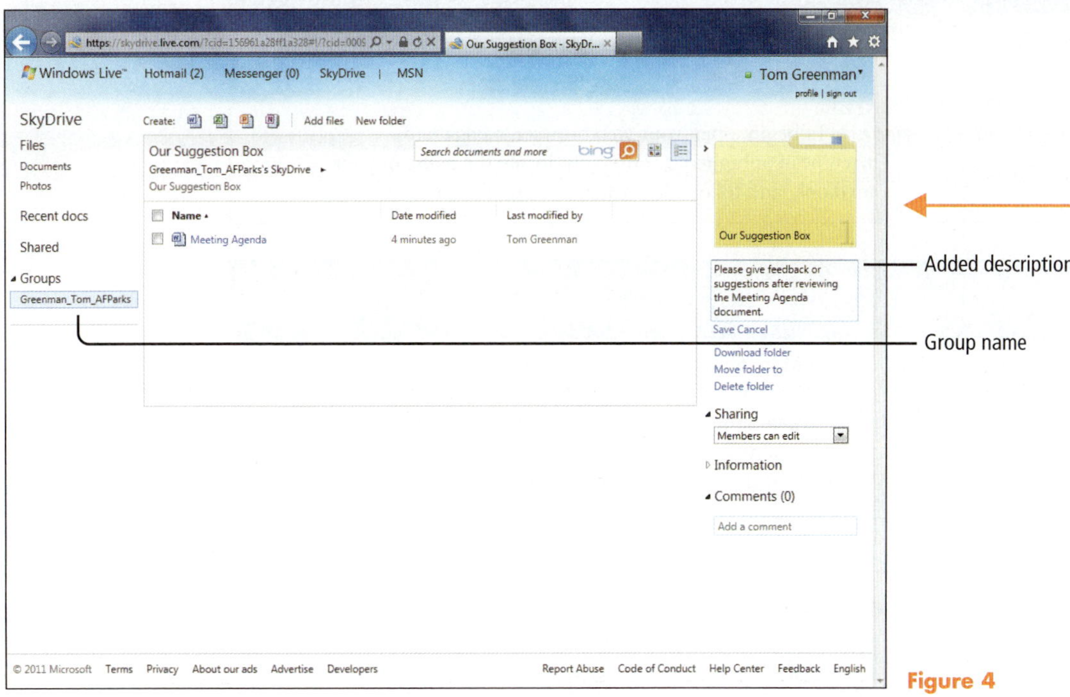

Figure 4

5. Click the folder and then click **Add** files. Click the **select them from your computer** link. Navigate to where you have stored your student data files. Click **wa01_Park_Meeting**, and then click the **Open** button. Click the **Continue** button. Compare your screen with **Figure 3**.
6. Click the **wa01_Park_Meeting** check box, and then click **Rename**.
7. Name the file Meeting Agenda and then press **Enter** and uncheck the file's check box.
8. In the right pane, click the **Add a description**.
9. In the **Add a description** box, type Please give feedback or suggestions after reviewing the Meeting Agenda document. Compare your screen with **Figure 4**, and then press **Enter**.
10. Click **Start**, click **All Programs**, and then click the **Accessories** folder. Click **Snipping Tool**, click the **New button arrow**, and then click **Full-screen Snip**.
11. Click the **Save Snip** button. In the **Save As** dialog box, navigate to your storage device. Open the **Web Apps Chapter 1** folder.
12. In the **File name** box, type Lastname_Firstname_wa01_Park_5 Verify that the **Save as type** box displays **JPEG file (*.JPG)**. Then click **Save**. **Close** the **Snipping Tool** window. Print the snips or submit the snips as directed by your instructor.

Done! **You have completed Skill 10 of 10**

More Skills

The following More Skills are located at **www.pearsonhighered.com/skills**

More Skills 11 Change Messenger Status

Messenger is a Windows Live service that can be used to send instant messages. You can control the visibility of your Messenger status within the Windows Live interface.

In More Skills 11, you will practice changing your Messenger status and observe the differences in the Messenger status indicator.

To begin, open your web browser, navigate to www.pearsonhighered.com/skills, locate the name of your textbook, and follow the instructions on the website.

More Skills 12 Set Dynamic Themes

Your Windows Live account can be personalized by adding a banner that displays at the top of each page.

In More Skills 12, you will set a dynamic theme to personalize your Windows Live account.

To begin, open your web browser, navigate to www.pearsonhighered.com/skills, locate the name of your textbook, and follow the instructions on the website.

More Skills 13 Create Personal Calendars

Windows Live provides an online calendaring system that can be used to schedule appointments, events, and track tasks.

In More Skills 13, you will create a calendar and share it with someone you trust. You will add to the To-do list and add an event.

To begin, open your web browser, navigate to www.pearsonhighered.com/skills, locate the name of your textbook, and follow the instructions on the website.

More Skills 14 Create Photo Albums

Photos can be stored in your Windows Live SkyDrive. This makes the photos accessible from any computer connected to the Internet.

In More Skills 14, you will upload photos to create a photo album. Then you will view the photos as a slide show.

To begin, open your web browser, navigate to www.pearsonhighered.com/skills, locate the name of your textbook, and follow the instructions on the website.

Key Terms

- **Breadcrumb trail** 11
- **CAPTCHA** 5
- **Cloud computing** 4
- **Folder** 10
- **Permissions** 16
- **Windows Live SkyDrive** 4
- **Snipping Tool** 6
- **Subfolder** 12
- **Windows Live** 4
- **Windows Live ID** 4

Online Help Skills

1. Start **Internet Explorer.** In the address bar, type explore.live.com/windows-live-skydrive-help-center and then press Enter to display the Windows Live SkyDrive Help Center page.
2. Near the middle of the page, below **Top solutions**, review the list of questions, and then click **What is SkyDrive?**
3. Read the article **What is Windows Live SkyDrive?,** and then see if you can answer the following question: How would you use the features of Windows Live SkyDrive to help you work on group projects?

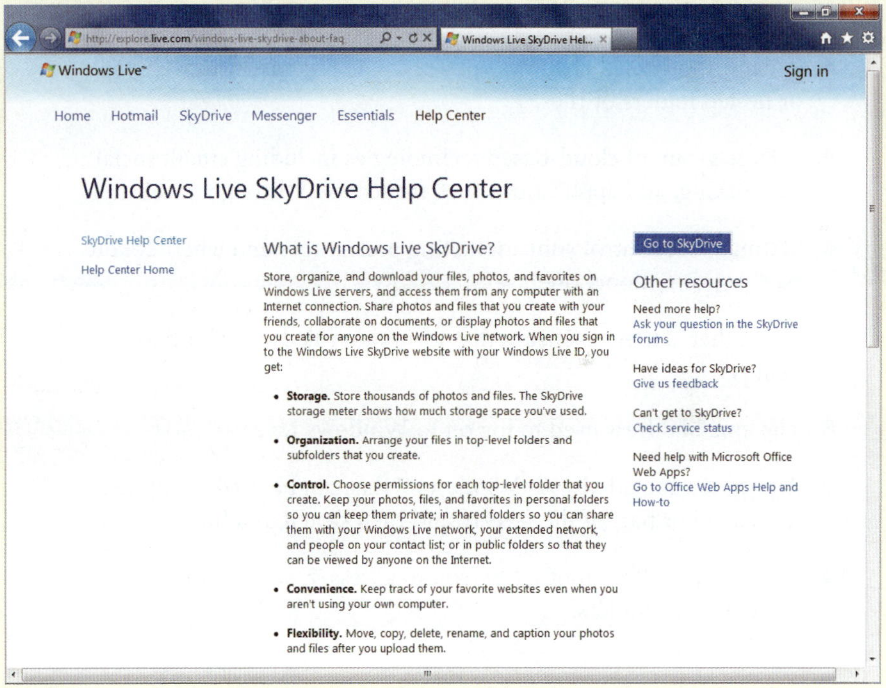

Figure 1

Matching

Match each term in the second column with its correct definition in the first column by writing the letter of the term on the blank line in front of the correct definition.

___ **1.** A service of Windows Live used to store, access, and share files and folders.

___ **2.** An Internet technology used to store files and to work with programs that are stored in a central location.

___ **3.** Settings that enable you to control who can search for you and access your profile.

___ **4.** A navigation bar that shows your place in a hierarchy of web pages or nested folders or files.

___ **5.** A large group of cloud-based technologies including email, social networking, and applications that are accessed through a website.

___ **6.** Settings that control your marketing preferences and whether you receive promotional offers.

___ **7.** A test that is used to ensure that forms are filled in by human beings.

___ **8.** The email address used to log on to Windows Live.

___ **9.** A program included with Windows 7 that can be used to capture the screen or part of the screen, and then save it as a file.

___ **10.** Settings that allow another person to access, read, modify, or delete files or folders.

A Account settings

B Breadcrumb trail

C CAPTCHA

D Cloud computing

E Permissions

F Privacy settings

G SkyDrive

H Snipping Tool

I Windows Live

J Windows Live ID

Multiple Choice

Choose the correct answer.

1. If you already have a(n) ___ and a password, then you are able to sign in to Windows Live.
   - A. Hotmail email address
   - B. available name
   - C. account setting
2. A strong password ___.
   - A. includes commonly used names or words
   - B. contains only uppercase letters
   - C. has 7 to 16 characters
3. A(n) ___ can be added to clarify the use or purpose of files or folders.
   - A. breadcrumb trail
   - B. account setting
   - C. description
4. After a folder is created, you can ___.
   - A. rename it but not move it
   - B. rename it and move it
   - C. not rename it, but you can move it
5. By default, folders and files in My Documents ___.
   - A. are automatically shared with Everyone (public)
   - B. are personal and are not shared with others
   - C. can be viewed and edited by Some friends
6. The folders on the Windows Live SkyDrive page are grouped according to their ___.
   - A. permissions
   - B. alphabetical order
   - C. groups
7. Sharing links by email or social networking sites is performed using ___.
   - A. viewed links
   - B. copied links
   - C. public links
8. A ___ can be created to share folders and files with others.
   - A. breadcrumb trail
   - B. privacy setting
   - C. group
9. Each group has its own website and ___.
   - A. email address
   - B. CAPTCHA
   - C. privacy statement
10. The group area where you can change roles or invite people to join is called ___.
    - A. Documents
    - B. Membership
    - C. Details

Topics for Discussion

1. In this chapter, you practiced sharing files with a public link. When would it be appropriate to share files using a public link? When would it not be appropriate, and why?
2. In this chapter, you learned to manage your Windows Live Profile. Is there any profile information that you do not want to share? Why?

Skill Check

To complete this project, you will need the following file:

- wa01_Market

You will save your snips as:

- Lastname_Firstname_wa01_Market_1
- Lastname_Firstname_wa01_Market_2

1. Start **Internet Explorer**, and then navigate to **live.com**.
2. Type your Windows Live ID and password, and then click the **Sign in** button. At the top of the page, click **SkyDrive**.
3. In the SkyDrive navigation bar, click **New folder**. In the **New folder** box, type Farmers' Market and then compare your screen with **Figure 1**.
4. Press **Enter**. Click the folder, and then **Add files**. Click **select them from your computer**.
5. Navigate to where you have stored your student data files, and then click **wa01_Market**. Click **Open**.
6. In the **Farmers' Market** folder, click the check box for **wa01_Market**, and then click **Rename**.
7. In the **New name** box, type Farmers' Market Flyer Press **Enter**, and then compare your screen with **Figure 2**.

■ Continue to the next page to complete this Skill Check

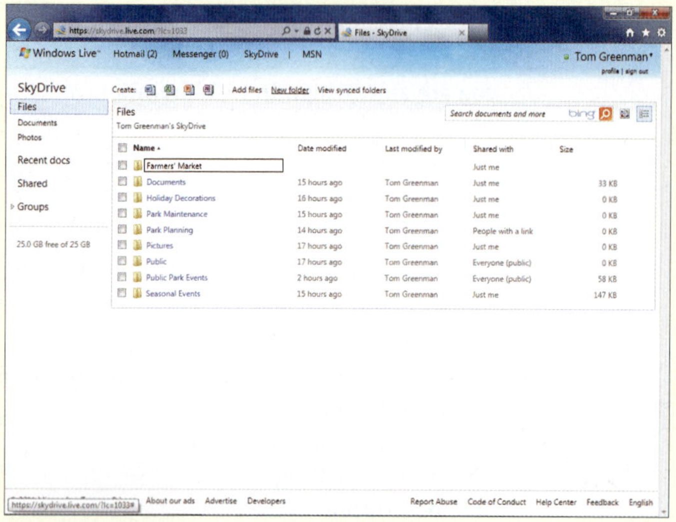

Figure 1

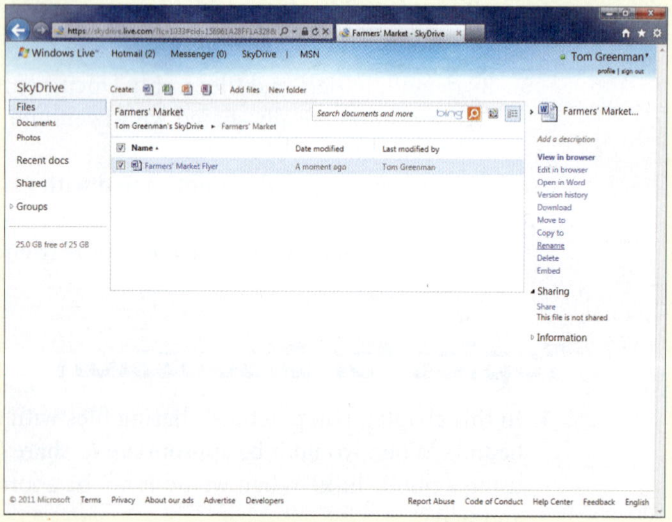

Figure 2

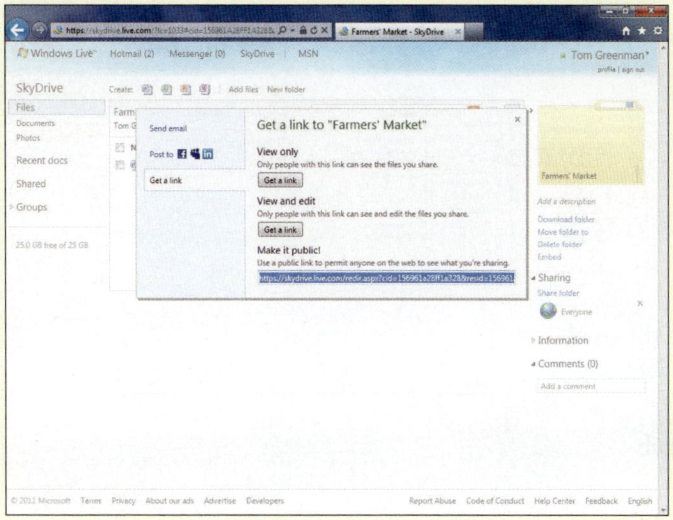

Figure 3

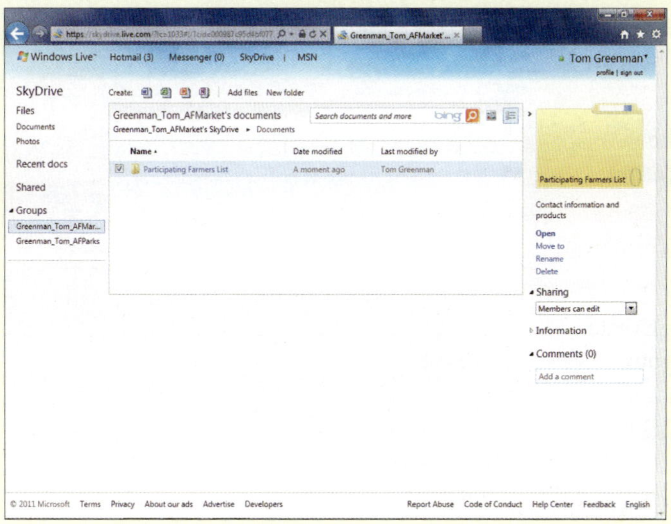

Figure 4

8. At the top of the page, click SkyDrive. Click the **Farmers' Market** folder. In the right pane, under Sharing, click **Share folder**.

9. Click **Get a link**. under **Make it public!**, click **Get a link**. Compare your screen with **Figure 3**.

10. Right-click the link and then click **Copy**. Click **Send email** and add your instructor's address. In the personal message box, right-click and then click **Paste**. Click **Share**.

11. Create a **Full-Screen snip**. Save the snip in your **Web Apps Chapter 1** folder as Lastname_Firstname_wa01_Market_1 and then **Close** the **Snipping Tool** window.

12. On the Windows Live navigation bar, point to **SkyDrive**, and then click **Groups**. Click **Create a group**.

13. In **the Name your group** box, type Lastname_Firstname_AFMarket and then click **Check availability**. If necessary, choose a different name.

14. In the **Add people** box, if your instructor provided an email address or list of email addresses to use in this project, type them with a comma between each address. Otherwise, type the email address of a friend you can trust.

15. Click the **Create** button, and if necessary, then click **Done**.

16. On the left side of the screen, click **Documents**.

17. On the SkyDrive navigation bar, click **New folder**, and then type Participating Farmers List Press **Enter**.

18. With the folder's check box selected, in the **Add a description** box, type Contact information and products Press **Enter** and then compare your screen with **Figure 4**.

19. Create a **Full-Screen snip**. **Save** the snip in your **Web Apps Chapter 1** folder as Lastname_Firstname_wa01_Market_2 and then **Close** the **Snipping Tool** window.

20. Sign out of **Windows Live**, and then close the browser window. Print or submit the snips as directed by your instructor.

Done! You have completed the Skill Check

Assess Your Skills 1

To complete this project, you will need the following file:

- wa01_Vacation

You will save your snips as:

- Lastname_Firstname_wa01_Vacation_1
- Lastname_Firstname_wa01_Vacation_2
- Lastname_Firstname_wa01_Vacation_3

1. Start **Internet Explorer**. Navigate to **live.com**, and then **sign on** to your Windows Live account.
2. Navigate to **SkyDrive**, and then create a new folder named Summer Travel
3. In the **Summer Travel** folder, create a subfolder named Vacation Checklist
4. In the **Vacation Checklist** folder, add the **wa01_Vacation** file located in the student files, and then rename the file as Vacation Planner
5. Change the permissions for the **Summer Travel** folder so that it can be accessed by Everyone. Send the link to your instructor. Compare your screen with **Figure 1**.
6. Create a **Full-screen snip**. Save the snip in your **Web Apps Chapter 1** folder as Lastname_Firstname_wa01_Vacation_1 **Close** the **Snipping Tool** window
7. Add the following description to the **Summer Travel** folder: Planning tools for your vacation time Compare your screen with **Figure 2**.
8. Create a **Full-screen snip**. **Save** the snip in your **Web Apps Chapter 1** folder as Lastname_Firstname_wa01_Vacation_2 **Close** the **Snipping Tool** window.
9. Add the following description to the **Vacation Checklist** folder: These are things you need to do to prepare for your upcoming vacation
10. In the **Summer Travel** folder, add a subfolder named **Vacation Itinerary**
11. For the **Vacation Itinerary** folder, add the following description: Here are the dates, names, addresses, and phone numbers where we will be staying.
12. In the **Summer Travel** folder, create a subfolder named Vacation Deals
13. For the **Vacation Deals** folder, add the following description: This is our vacation budget.
14. Rename the **Vacation Deals** folder as Vacation Budget
15. Return to the **Summer Travel** folder. Create a **Full-screen snip**. **Save** the snip in your **Web Apps Chapter 1** folder as Lastname_Firstname_wa01_Vacation_3 **Close** the **Snipping Tool** window.
16. Sign out of Windows Live, and then **Close** the browser window. Print or submit the snips as directed by your instructor.

Done! You have completed Assess Your Skills 1

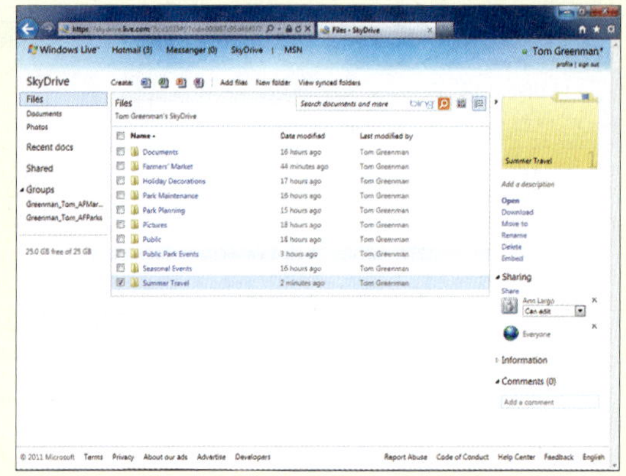

Figure 1

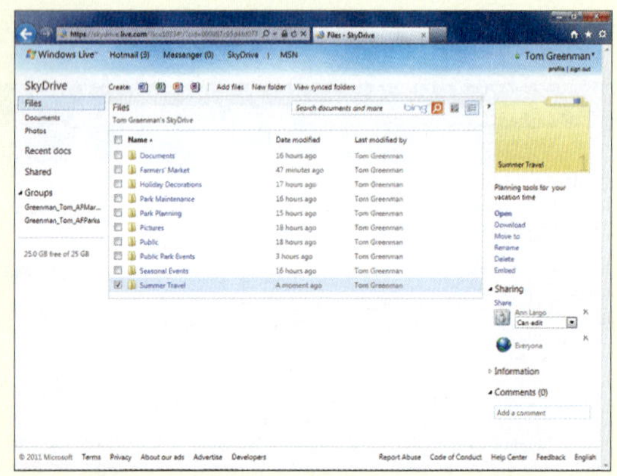

Figure 2

Assess Your Skills 2

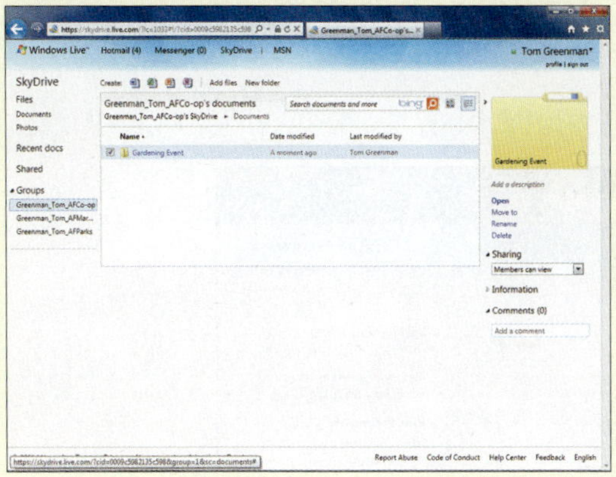

Figure 1

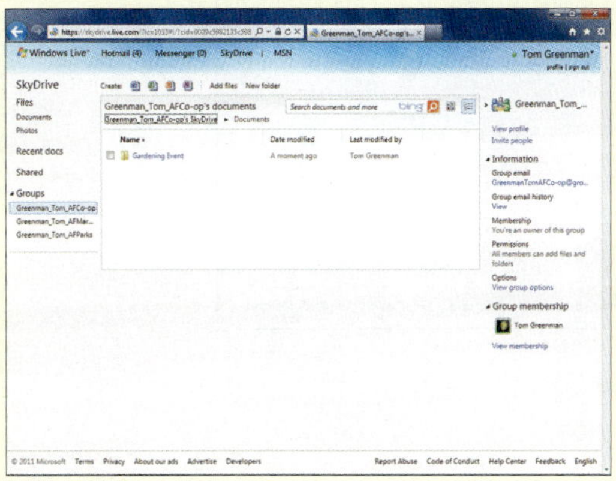

Figure 2

To complete this project, you will need the following file:

- **wa01_Co-op**

You will save your snips as:

- **Lastname_Firstname_wa01_Co-op_1**
- **Lastname_Firstname_wa01_Co-op_2**

1. Start **Internet Explorer**. Navigate to **live.com**, and then sign on to your Windows Live account.
2. Create a new Windows Live group named **Lastname_Firstname_AFCo-op**
3. Invite your instructor, a list of members provided by your instructor, or a friend that you can trust to the group.
4. In your group's Documents, create a folder named Gardening Event
5. Change the permissions for the folder so that **Members can view**. Compare your screen with **Figure 1**.
6. Create a **Full-screen snip**. **Save** the snip in your **Web Apps Chapter 1** folder as Lastname_Firstname_wa01_Co-op_1 Close the **Snipping Tool** window.
7. Add the file **wa01_Co-op** to the **Gardening Event** folder, and then rename the file as Gardening Event Flyer
8. For the **Gardening Event** folder, type the following description: All vegetables grown at the AF Co-op Garden will be donated to the local Food Bank.
9. Return to the **Lastname_Firstname_AFCo-op** group page.
10. In your group's Documents, create a folder named Co-op Membership Drive
11. Return to the **Lastname_Firstname_AFCo-op** Documents. Compare your screen with **Figure 2**.
12. Create a **Full-screen snip**. **Save** the snip in your **Web Apps Chapter 1** folder as Lastname_Firstname_wa01_Co-op_2 **Close** the **Snipping Tool** window.
13. Sign out of **Windows Live**, and then **Close** the browser window. Print or submit the snips as directed by your instructor.

Done! You have completed Assess Your Skills 2

Assess Your Skills Visually

To complete this project, you will need the following file:

- wa01_Picnic

You will save your snip as:

- **Lastname_Firstname_wa01_Picnic**

Create a SkyDrive folder as shown in **Figure 1**. The folder's name is **Family Picnic**, with sharing set to **Everyone**. The **Family Picnic** folder contains a subfolder named **Flyers** that stores the file **wa01_Picnic**, which has been uploaded from the student data files. The document has been renamed to **Picnic Flyer**. A description has been added to the file.

Compare your screen with **Figure 1**, and then create a **Full-screen snip** and save the snip as Lastname_Firstname_wa01_Picnic Save the snip in your **Web Apps Chapter 1** folder. **Close** the **Snipping Tool** window. Print the snip or submit the snip as directed by your instructor.

Done! You have completed Assess Your Skills Visually

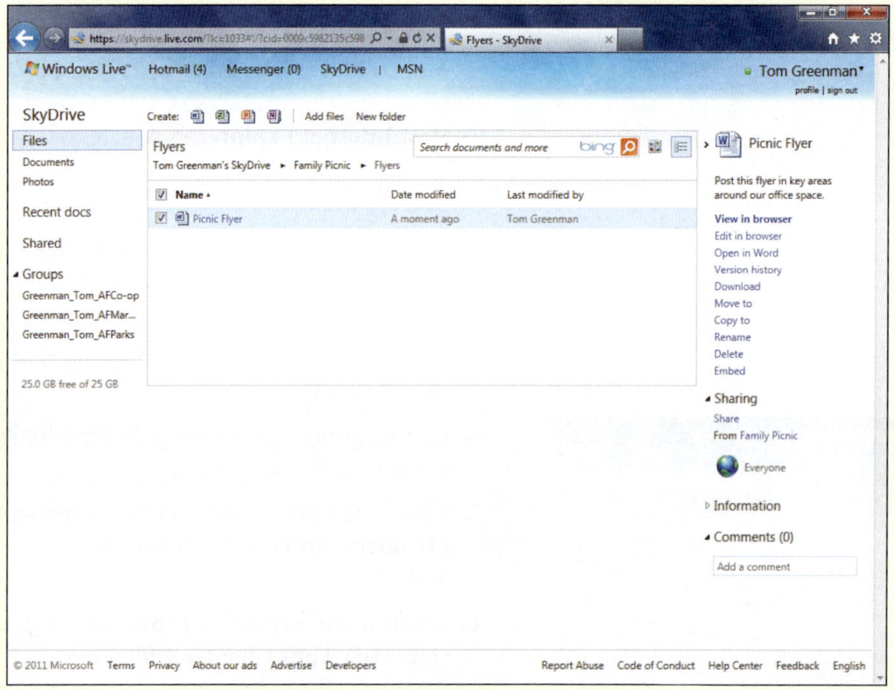

Figure 1

Skills in Context

To complete this project, you will need the following file:

- **wa01_Advisory**

You will save your snips as:

- **Lastname_Firstname_wa01_Advisory_1**
- **Lastname_Firstname_wa01_Advisory_2**

The Aspen Falls Parks and Recreation Department needs to create an advisory board made up of the community's citizens, local school administrators, and potential corporate sponsors. Now more than ever, partnerships between public and private sectors are necessary to develop a thriving community. The board's goal is to brainstorm year-round programs that utilize the city's park and recreation facilities. Use the skills you have practiced in this chapter to create a group for the advisory board to use as its collaboration tool. Choose an appropriate name for the group. Invite two classmates or people that you trust to join the group.

Create at least three folders that you think the group will need to complete its goal. Then, add a description for two of the folders so that each member of the group will know how to use the folder. Create a **Full-screen snip** named Lastname_Firstname_wa01_Advisory_1

Upload **wa01_Advisory** to one of the folders. Rename the file Advisory Board Meeting Notes Create a **Full-screen snip** named Lastname_Firstname_wa01_Advisory_2 Print the snips or submit the snips as directed by your instructor.

Done! You have completed Skills in Context

Skills and You

To complete this project, you will need the following file:

- **None**

You will save your snip as:

- **Lastname_Firstname_wa01_Profile**

Use the skills you have practiced in this chapter to edit your Windows Live profile and privacy settings. Develop your profile so that it is a reflection of you that can be shared with anyone on a professional, not personal, level.

Review your Contact info, Work info, Social info, and Education info to be sure that your personal safety is protected.

Document your work by creating a **Full-screen snip**. Save the snip in your **Web Apps Chapter 1** folder as Lastname_Firstname_wa01_Profile Print the snip or submit the snip as directed by your instructor.

Done! You have completed Skills and You

CHAPTER 2

Getting Started with Office Web Apps

- Office Web Apps contains web-based versions of Word, Excel, PowerPoint, and OneNote.
- Documents, workbooks, presentations, and notebooks can be created, saved, and modified in a web browser and stored in your Windows Live SkyDrive.
- Using SkyDrive and Office Web Apps, you can open and edit your Office files using a web browser. Microsoft Office does not need to be installed on your computer.
- Office Web Apps files can be shared by setting permissions or by sharing links to the files.
- Graphics can be added to Office Web Apps documents and files.

Alexander Kirch/Shutterstock

Aspen Falls City Hall

In this chapter, you will use Office Web Apps to create documents for the Aspen Falls Parks and Recreation Department, which provides recreational facilities and services for the citizens and visitors of Aspen Falls, California. You will assist Tom Greenman, Supervisor, to create and edit documents using Office Web Apps.

You will work with documents, workbooks, presentations, and notebooks while applying skills common to all Office Web Apps programs. You will also insert graphics into Office Web Apps documents.

Time to complete all 10 skills – 60 to 90 minutes

Student data file needed for this chapter:

New blank Office Web App documents

You will save your snips as:

Lastname_Firstname_wa02_Gardens_1
Lastname_Firstname_wa02_Gardens_2
Lastname_Firstname_wa02_Gardens_3
Lastname_Firstname_wa02_Gardens_4
Lastname_Firstname_wa02_Gardens_5

Outcome

Using the skills in this chapter, you will be able to work with Office Web Apps documents like this:

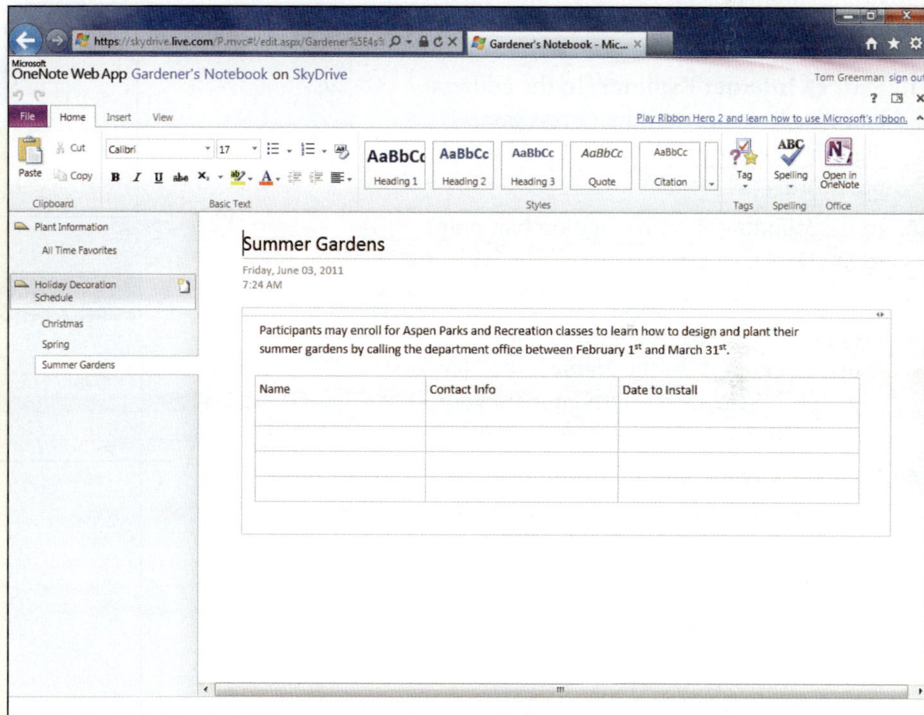

SKILLS

At the end of this chapter you will be able to:

Skill 1 Create Documents in Word Web App
Skill 2 Edit Documents in Word Web App
Skill 3 Share Word Web App Documents
Skill 4 Create Workbooks in Excel Web App
Skill 5 Modify Workbooks in Excel Web App
Skill 6 Create Presentations in PowerPoint Web App
Skill 7 Enhance Presentations in PowerPoint Web App
Skill 8 Create Notebooks in OneNote Web App
Skill 9 Add Content to Notebooks in OneNote Web App
Skill 10 Use Office Web Apps to Insert Graphics

MORE SKILLS

Skill 11 Edit Files Stored in SkyDrive in Word
Skill 12 Create Excel Web App Charts
Skill 13 Insert Graphics in OneNote Web App Notebooks
Skill 14 Download SkyDrive Files to Your Computer

- ▸ ***Office Web Apps*** are Web-based versions of Microsoft Office programs (Word, Excel, PowerPoint, and OneNote) that are available online through Windows Live.
- ▸ When you work with Office documents using a Web App, you open, edit, and format the documents in a web browser. That is, the Office application is not used and does not need to be installed on your computer.
- ▸ ***Word Web App*** is the word-processing application used to create documents that is available as part of Office Web Apps.
- ▸ Recall that documents stored on SkyDrive can be shared with others.

1. Start **Internet Explorer**. In the address bar, type live.com and then press Enter. Sign in using your Windows Live ID and password.
2. In the Windows Live navigation bar, point to **SkyDrive**. Compare your screen with **Figure 1**.
3. From the **SkyDrive** menu, click **New Word document**. In the **Name**, type New Employee Welcome Letter Compare your screen with **Figure 2**.
4. Click the **Create** button. If prompted by an *Improve Your Experience* information message, click the **Close** button.

■ **Continue to the next page to complete the skill**

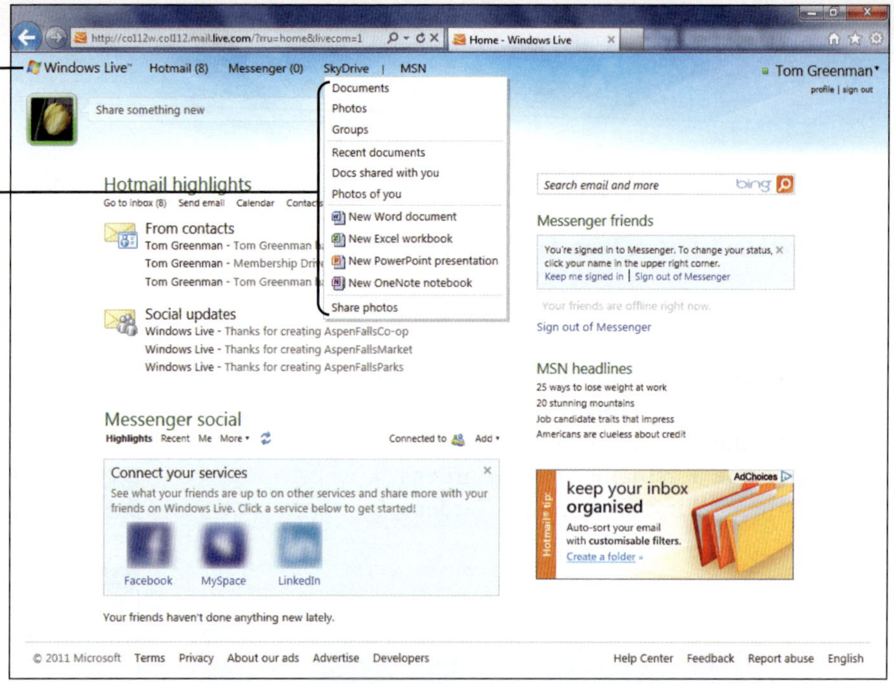

Figure 1

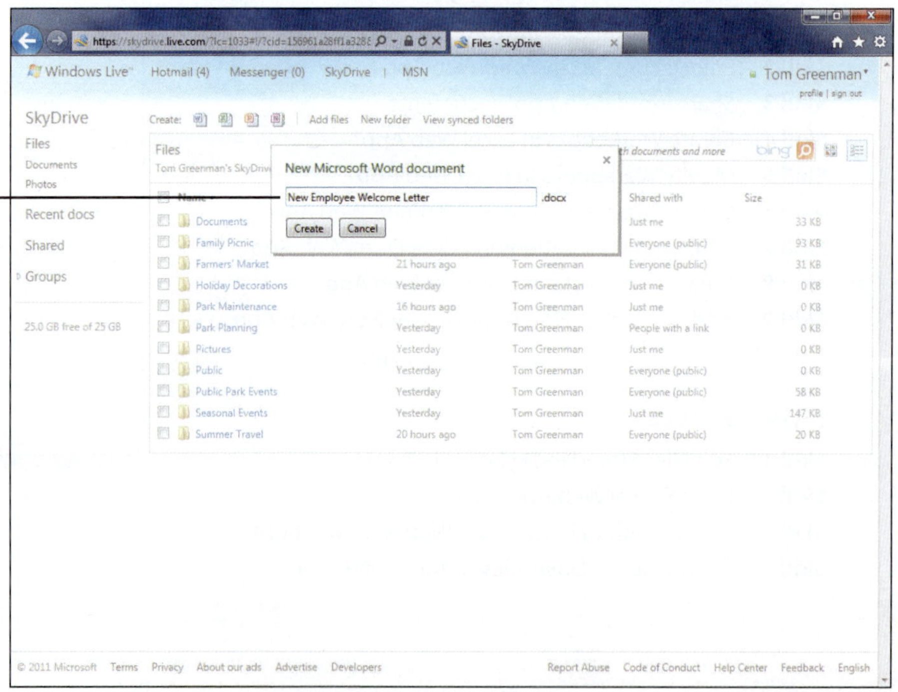

Figure 2

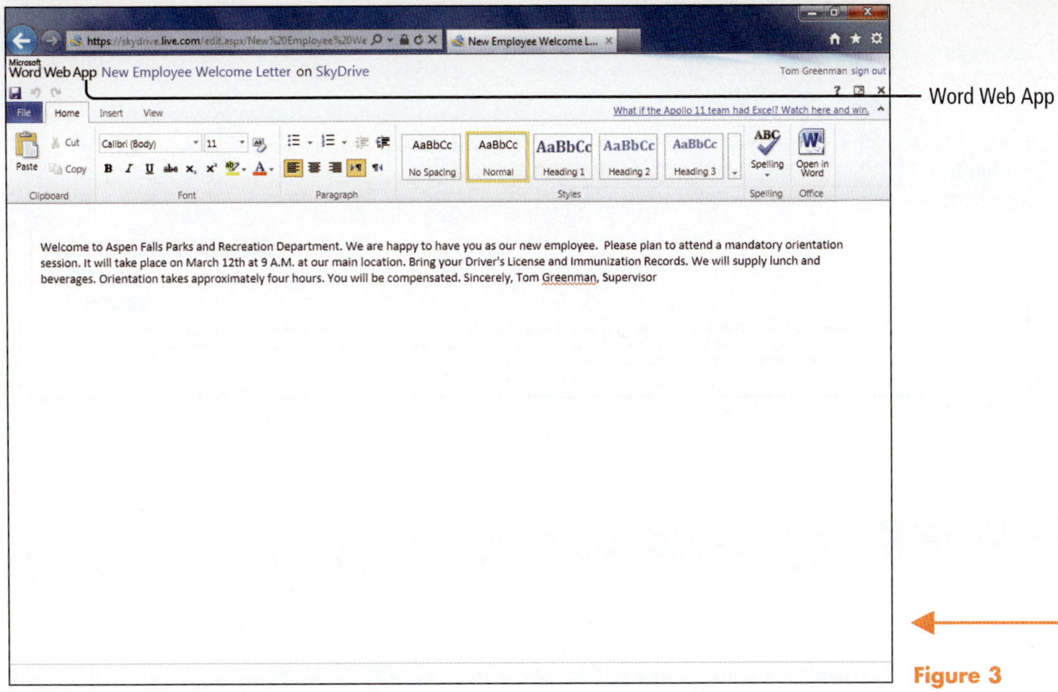

Figure 3

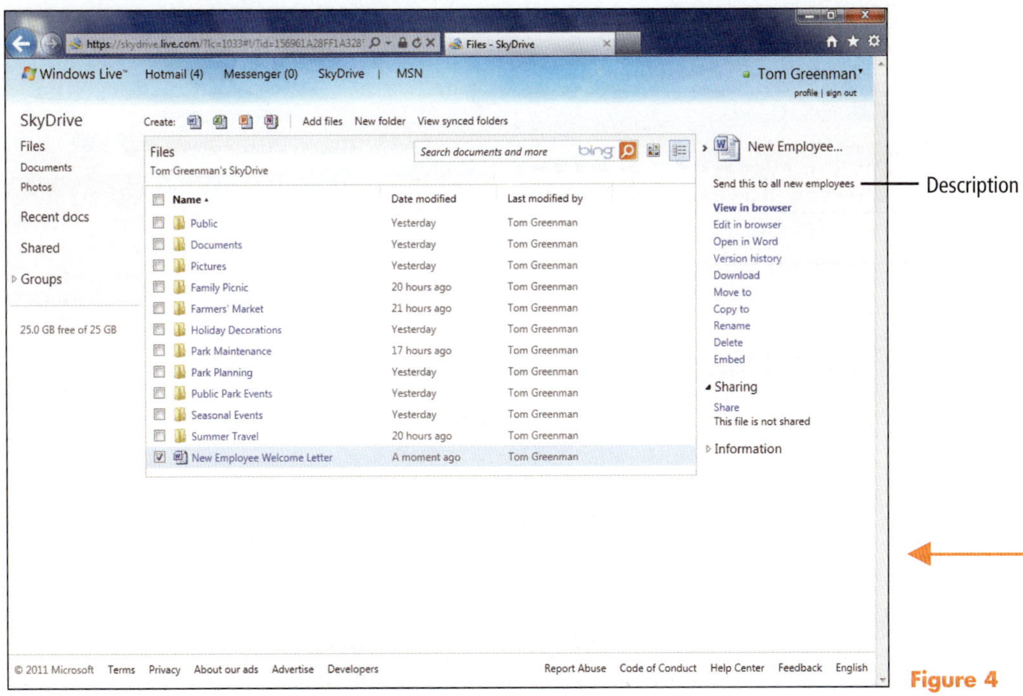

Figure 4

5. In the new, blank document, type Welcome to Aspen Falls Parks and Recreation Department. We are happy to have you as our new employee. Please plan to attend a mandatory orientation session. It will take place on March 12th at 9 A.M. at our main location. Bring your Driver's License and Immunization Records. We will supply lunch and beverages. Orientation takes approximately four hours. You will be compensated. Sincerely, Tom Greenman, Supervisor Click the **Save button**.

6. On the **View tab**, click **Reading View**. If prompted by an *Improve Your Experience* information message, click the **Close** button. Read the letter, and then click **Edit in Browser** to return to Editing View. **Save** the file. Compare your screen with **Figure 3**.

   You cannot make changes to the document in Reading view. The Ribbon is not visible. In Editing view the Ribbon is visible, and you can continue making changes to the document.

7. On the **Home tab**, in the **Spelling group**, click the top half of the **Spelling** button. Correct any spelling errors, and then click **Save**.

   Proper names, such as Greenman, may not be in the Spelling dictionary and may be marked as incorrectly spelled. Check names carefully for errors.

8. On the **File tab**, click **Close**. If a message displays about navigating away from the page, click **Leave this page**.

9. On the right, just below the document name, click **Add a description**. Type Send this to all new employees Click **Save**, and then compare your screen with **Figure 4**. Keep SkyDrive open for the next skill.

■ **You have completed Skill 1 of 10**

- Using the Word Web App, you can edit Word documents in a browser, and you can add bullets, change alignment, check spelling, and perform other tasks.
- When bold, italic, or font color is added to a word, it is referred to as ***formatting***.

1. In the New Employee Welcome Letter properties pane, click **Edit in browser**.
2. With the insertion point to the left of the word *Welcome*, type Aspen Falls Parks and Recreation Department Press Enter, and then type 500 S Aspen Street Press Enter, type Aspen Falls, CA 93463 and then press Enter.
3. Position the mouse to the left of the first line that begins with *Aspen* and drag over all the text, ending at 93463. Release the left mouse button. This will select the first three lines of text.
4. With the three lines selected, on the **Home tab**, in the **Paragraph group**, click the **Align Text Right** button. Click the **Save** button. Compare your screen with **Figure 1**.
5. Position the insertion point to the left of the word *Welcome*. Type Dear Applicant, and then press Enter.
6. Select the text *Welcome to Aspen Falls Parks and Recreation Department*. In the **Font group**, click the **Italic** button. Click the **Font Color** button arrow, and then under **Standard Colors**, click the sixth color—**Dark Green**.
7. After the word *Department*, replace the period with an exclamation point. Click the **Save** button, and then compare your screen with **Figure 2**.
8. In the third sentence, position the insertion point to the left of the word *Please*, and then press Enter.

■ Continue to the next page to complete the skill

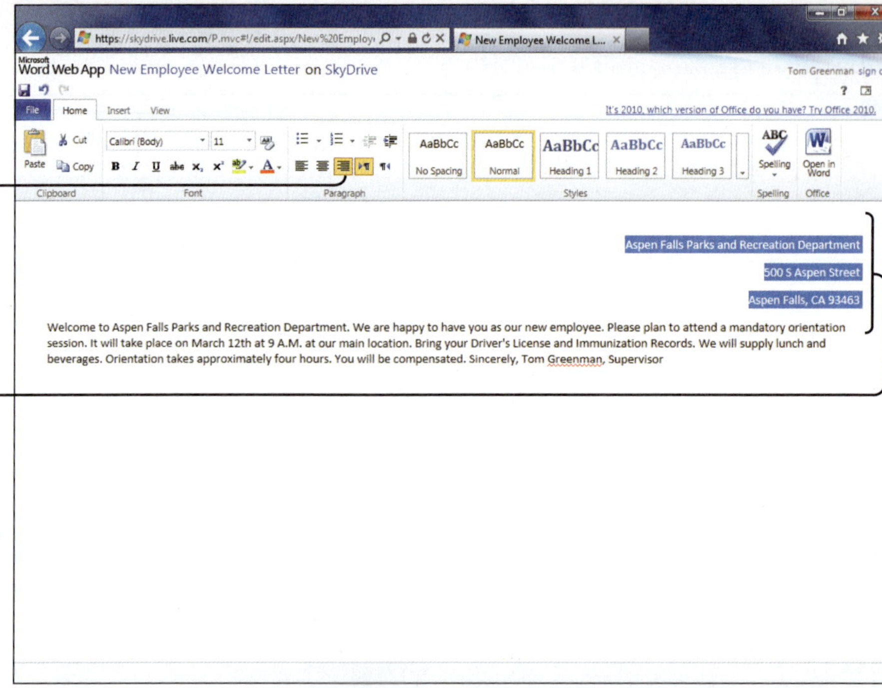

Figure 1

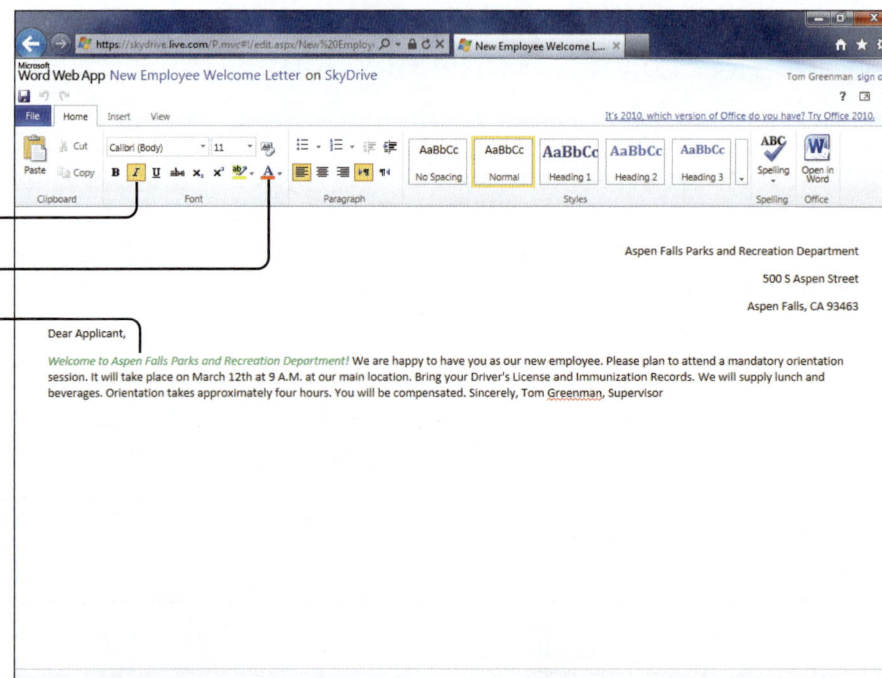

Figure 2

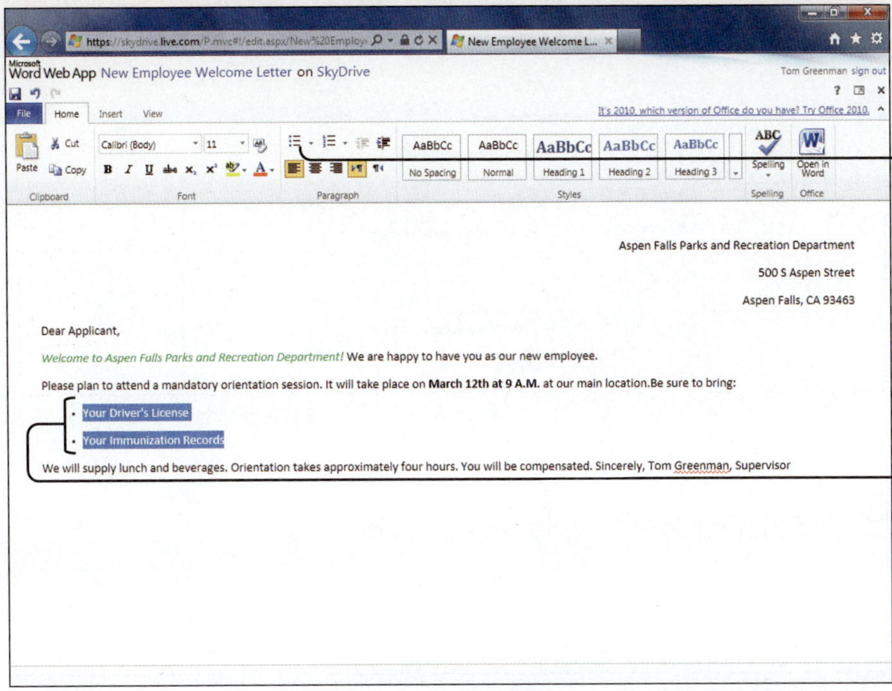

Figure 3

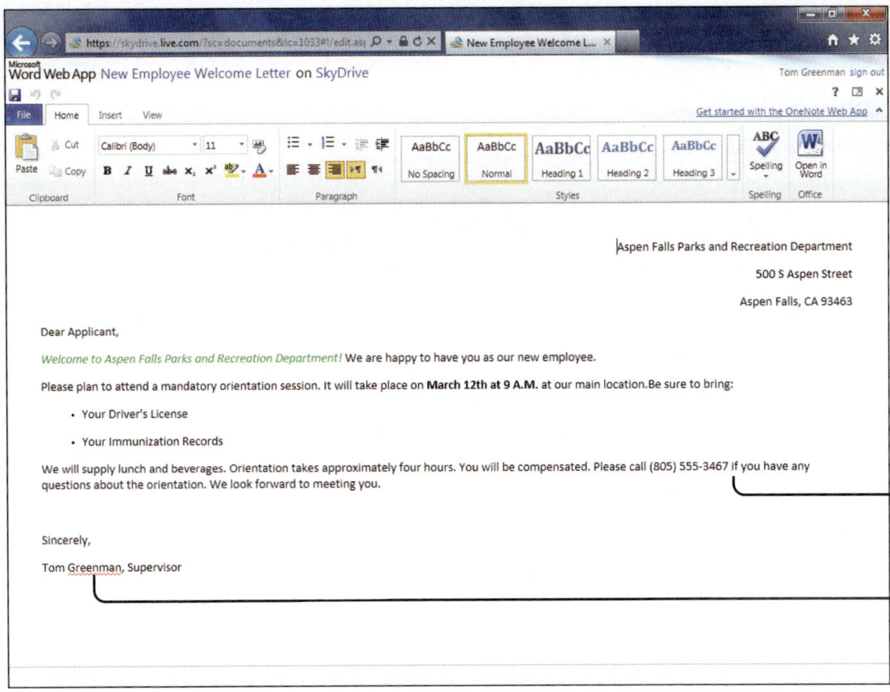

Figure 4

9. In the fourth sentence, select the text *March 12th at 9 A.M.* In the **Font group**, click the **Bold** button, then click the **Save** button.
10. In the fifth sentence, position the insertion point to the left of the word *Bring*. Type Be sure to In the word *Bring*, change the capital *B* to a lowercase b After the word *bring*, type : (a colon), and then press Enter.
11. In the fifth sentence, position the insertion point to the left of the word *your* and change the lowercase *y* to an uppercase Y Position the insertion point after the word *License*, and then press Enter.
12. In the fifth sentence, position the insertion point to the left of the word *Immunization*, and then replace the word *and* with the word Your After the word *Records*, delete the period and the space, and then press Enter. Select the two lines that begin with *Your*. In the **Paragraph group**, click the **Bullets button arrow**, and then click **Square Bullet**.
13. Click the **Save** button, and then compare your screen with **Figure 3**.
14. Position the insertion point to the left of the word *Sincerely*, and then press Enter two times. Position the insertion point to the left of the word *Tom*, and then press Enter.
15. Position the insertion point after *compensated*, and type Please call (805) 555-3467 if you have any questions about the orientation. We look forward to meeting you. Click the **Save** button, and then compare your screen with **Figure 4**.
16. On the **File tab**, click **Close** to exit the Word Web App and display the file in SkyDrive.

■ **You have completed Skill 2 of 10**

- You can control who accesses your SkyDrive documents by setting the sharing permissions of the document.
- You can also control whether the document can be viewed or edited.
- A link to a document can be sent via email using the Send a link command.

1. On the SkyDrive page, in the SkyDrive navigation bar, to the right of *Create*, click **Create Word document**. In the **Name**, type Schedule Request Form
2. Click the **Create** link. Click the **File** tab and then click **Share**. Compare your screen with **Figure 1**.
3. Type your instructor's email address and then click the **Share** button to return to the document in Word Web App.
4. Type Please fill out this form and return it to Tom Greenman, Supervisor. Scheduling requests must be made at least two weeks in advance. Press Enter two times.
5. On the **Insert tab**, click the **Table** button, and then position the mouse two columns to the right and three rows down. Click the left mouse button to insert a 2 × 3 table. Compare your screen with **Figure 2**.
6. Point to the right side of the table, and then, using the **Horizontal Resize** mouse pointer, drag to the right to make the table span the screen so that it is just beyond the end of the sentences above the table.
7. In the first row of the first column, type Dates requested: In the second row of the first column, type Name: In the third row of the first column, type Reason for request:

■ Continue to the next page to complete the skill

Share dialog box

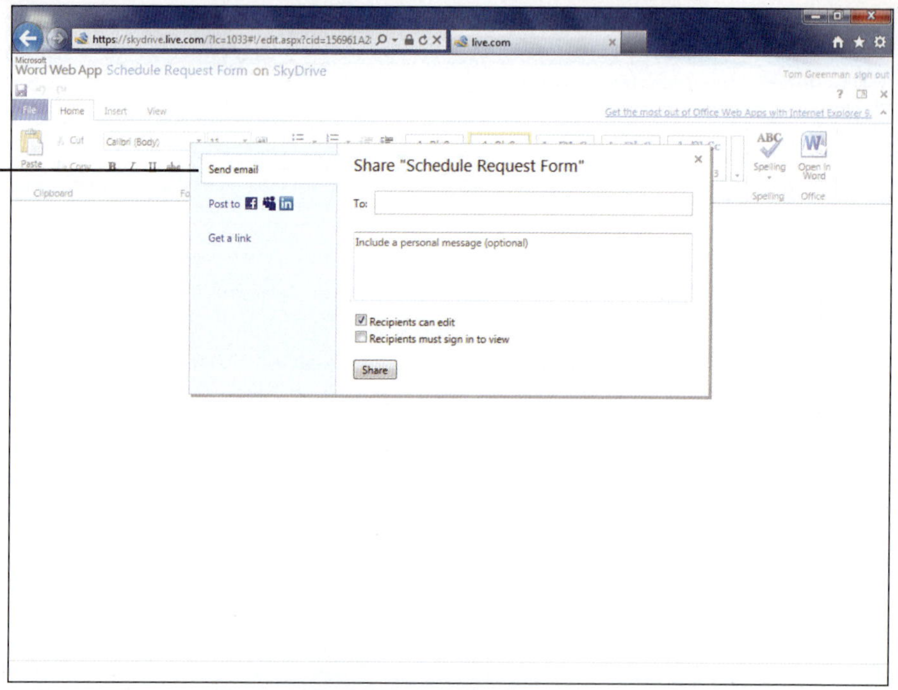

Figure 1

Table button

2x3 table inserted

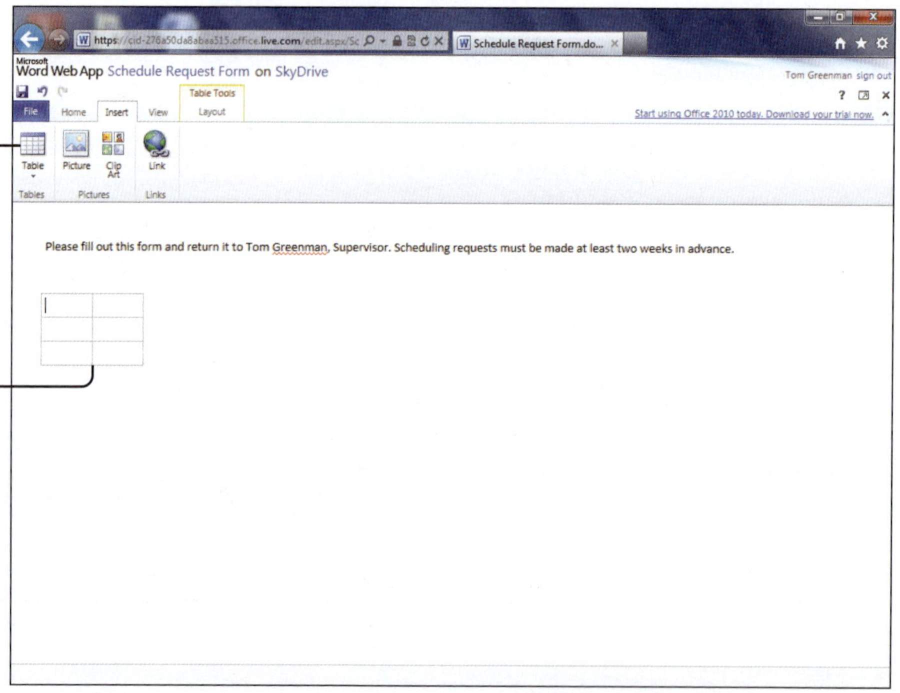

Figure 2

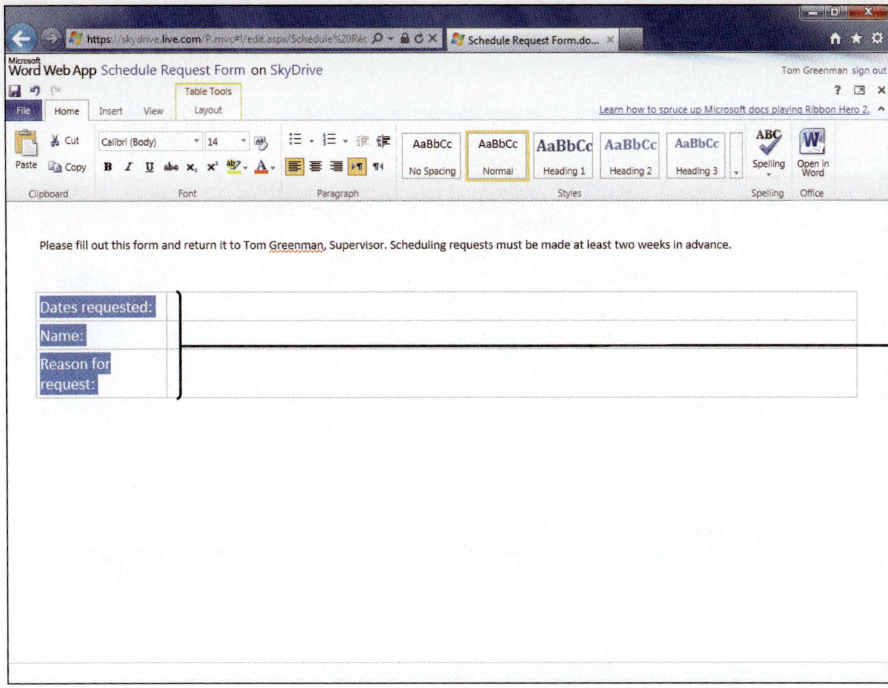

Text added and formatted

Figure 3

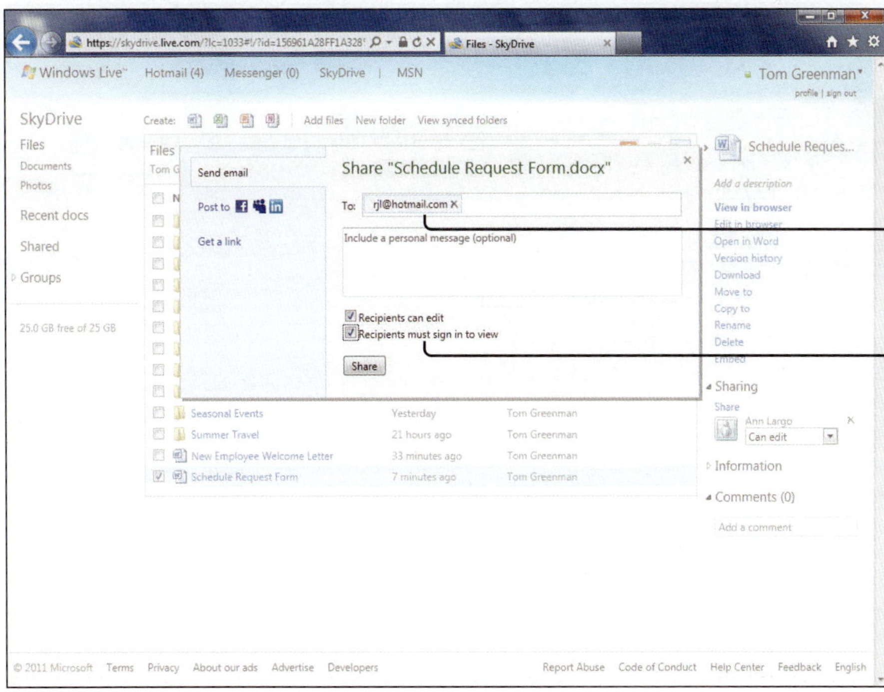

E-mail address that link will be sent to

Require recipients to sign in with Windows Live ID check box selected

Figure 4

8. On the **Layout tab**, in the **Select group**, click **Select Column**. Click the **Home tab**. In the **Font group**, click the **Font Size** arrow, and then click **14**. Compare your screen with **Figure 3**.
9. Click in the last table cell. On the **Layout tab**, in the **Insert group**, click **Insert Below**. In the fourth row of the first column, type Have you asked anyone to trade with you? If necessary, select the text and keep the **Font Size** at **11**.
10. Click the **Save** button, and then on the **File tab**, click **Close** to return to SkyDrive.

    The Sharing section shows with whom the document is shared.
11. On the right, under Sharing, click **Share**.
12. On the **Send an email** option, in the **To** box, type the email address of a friend you can trust. Select the **Recipients must sign in to view** check box, and then compare your screen with **Figure 4**.

    A link to the Schedule Request Form will be sent to the email address that you typed. The recipient can view the form only after he or she signs in to Windows Live.
13. Create a **Full-screen snip**. Navigate to your storage device and create a folder named Web Apps Chapter 2 Name the snip Lastname_Firstname_wa02_Gardens_1 and save it as a JPEG file (*.jpg) in the folder.
14. Click the **Share** button. Wait a few moments, and when you return to SkyDrive, look on the right of the page for verification that the file has been shared.

■ **You have completed Skill 3 of 10**

- *Excel Web App* is the part of Office Web Apps used to work with Excel workbooks and worksheets.
- A ***workbook*** is an Excel file that contains one or more worksheets. A ***worksheet*** is used in Excel to store and work with data.
- Data can be entered into ***cells***—the location where one column and one row intersect.

1. On the SkyDrive page, in the SkyDrive navigation bar, to the right of *Create*, click **Create Excel workbook**. Compare your screen with **Figure 1**.
2. In the **Name**, type Inventory Orders Click the **Create** button.
3. If the *Improve Your Experience* information message appears, click the **Close** button [×].
4. In cell **A1**, type Inventory Orders by Plant Category and then press Enter.
5. In cell **A2**, type Replacement Plants and New Plantings and then press Enter two times.
6. In cell **A4**, type Trees and then press Tab. In cell **B4**, type Shrubs and then press Tab. In cell **C4**, type Bulbs and then press Tab. In cell **D4**, type Annuals and then press Tab. In cell **E4**, type Total Orders and then press Tab twice. Compare your screen with **Figure 2**.

   Cell E4 has automerged or automatically become a merged cell in order to accommodate the content. In Excel Web App, you can wrap the text as another option to keep the content within one cell. A second alternative is to adjust the column width by dragging the column border.

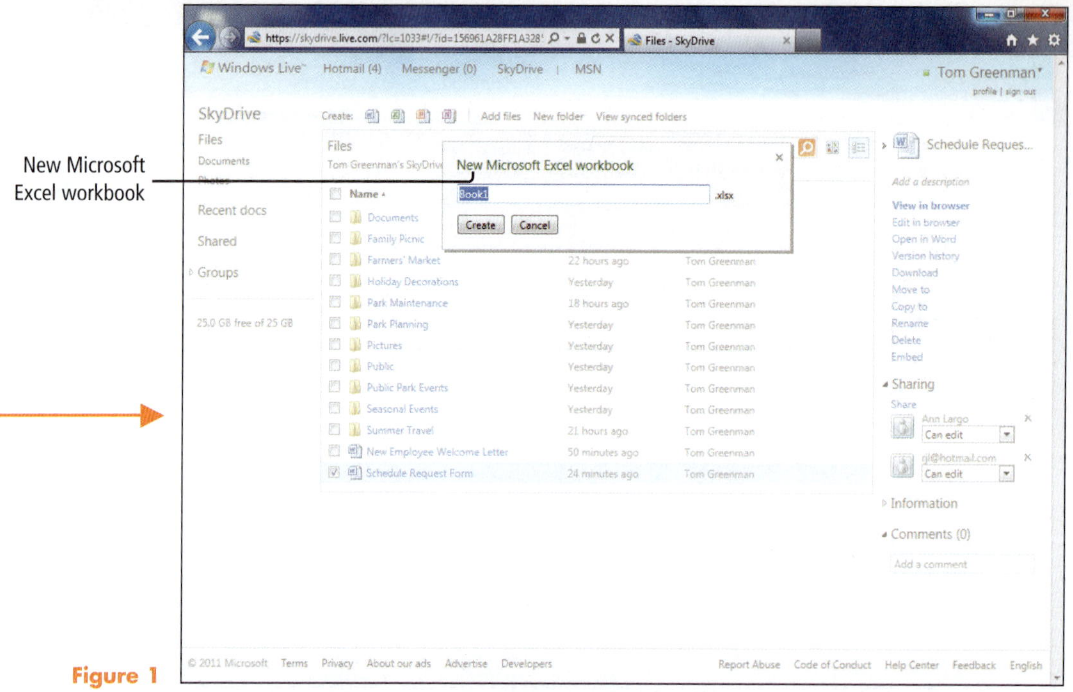

Figure 1

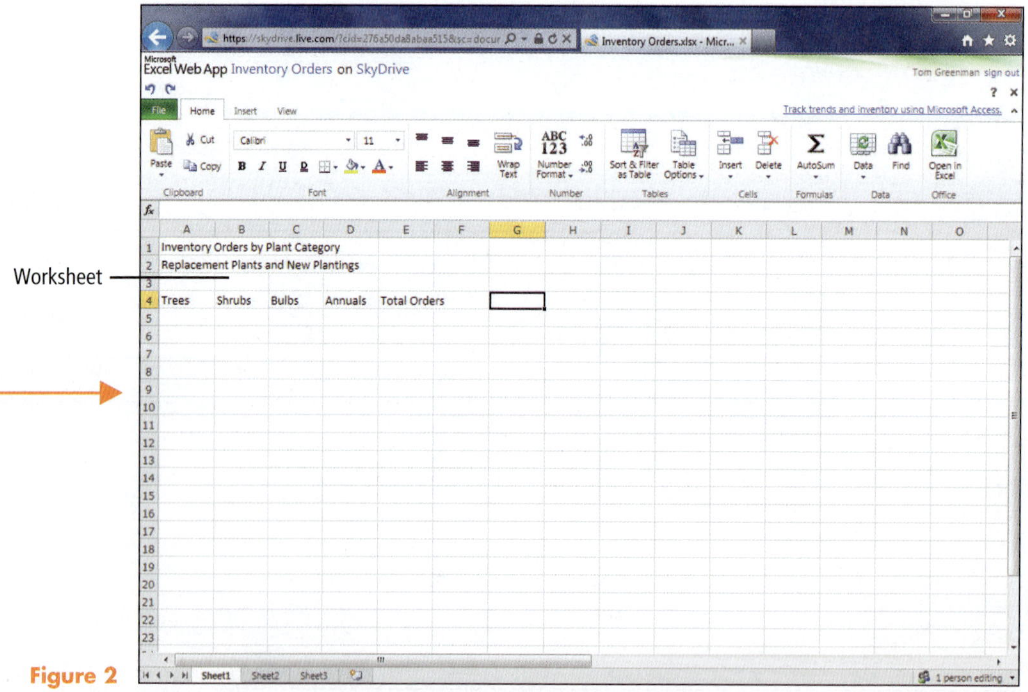

Figure 2

■ Continue to the next page to complete the skill

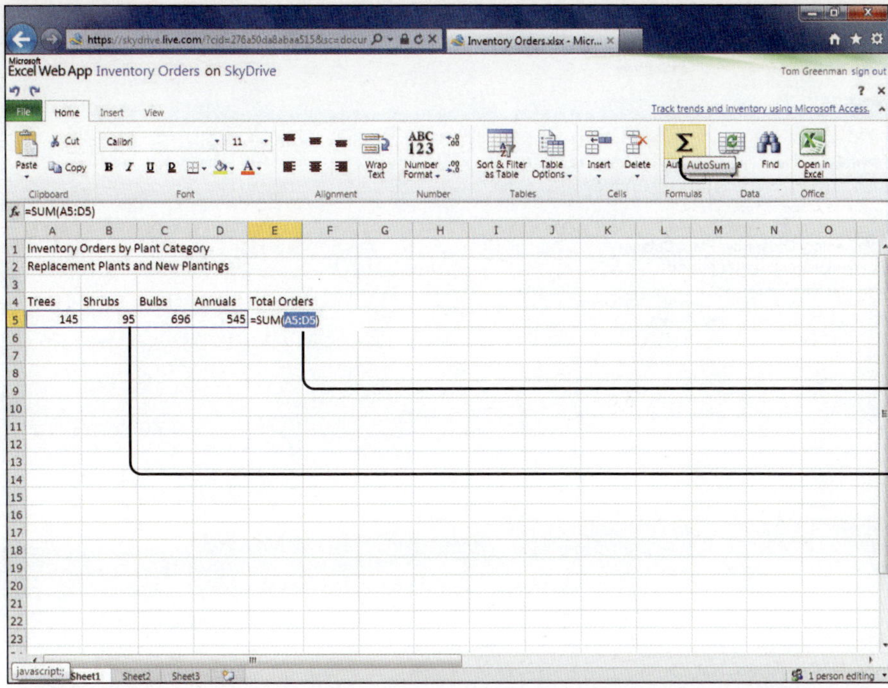

Figure 3

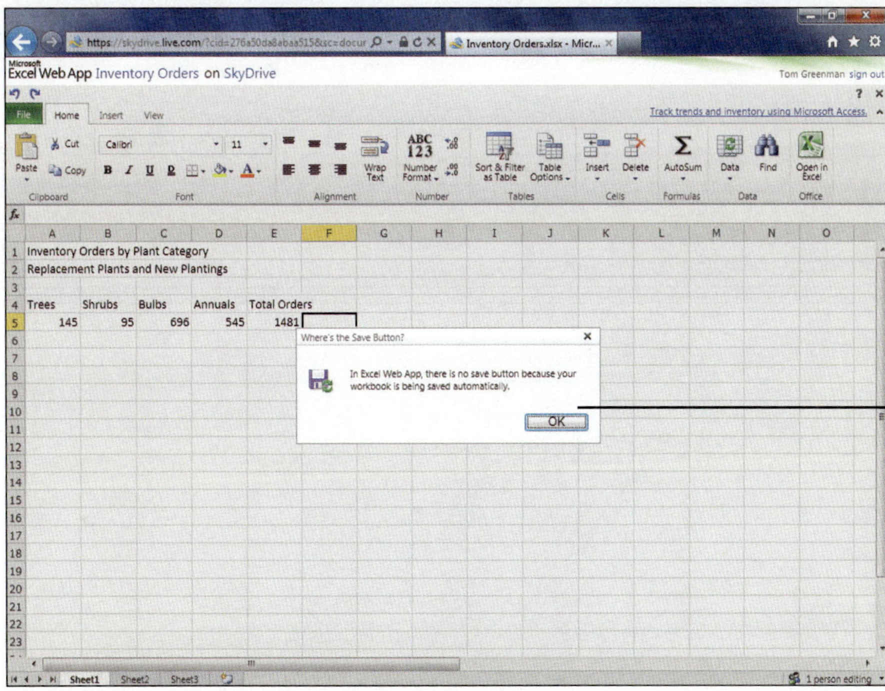

Figure 4

7. Click cell **A5**, type 145 and then press Tab. In cell **B5**, type 95 and then press Tab. In cell **C5**, type 696 and then press Tab. In cell **D5**, type 545 and then press Tab.
8. With the insertion point in cell **E5**, on the **Home tab**, in the **Formulas group**, click the top half of the **AutoSum** button, and then compare your screen with **Figure 3**.

   AutoSum is an Excel feature used to insert prewritten functions into a cell. A ***function*** performs mathematical calculations according to cell references and values in their parenthesis. Here, the SUM function totals the values in the range A5:D5.

   A ***cell reference*** identifies the cell location by listing the column first and then listing the row.
9. Press Tab to accept the SUM function.

   The total amount of orders—1481—displays.
10. Click the **File tab**, click **Where's the Save Button?**, and then compare your screen with **Figure 4**.

    Excel Web App automatically saves your work so there is no need for a Save button.
11. In the **Where's the Save Button** dialog box, click the **OK** button. Keep the workbook open for the next skill.

■ **You have completed Skill 4 of 10**

- An entire row or column can be selected by clicking the row number or column letter.
- A cell's ***value***—its data—can be formatted by changing font type, size, and color.
- New rows and columns can be inserted into a worksheet.

1. In the **Inventory Orders** workbook, on the left edge of the worksheet, click the number **1** to select the entire row. In the **Font group**, click the **Font arrow**, and then click **Helvetica**. Click the **Font Size arrow**, and then click **14**. Compare your screen with **Figure 1**.
2. Repeat the technique just practiced to select row **2**. In the **Font group**, click the **Font arrow**, and then click **Helvetica**. Click the **Font Size** arrow, and then click **12**. Click the **Italic** button.
3. Select row **4**, and then in the **Font group**, click the **Font Color arrow**. Under Standard Colors, click **Blue**, and then click the **Bold** button. Click the **Font** arrow, and then click **Helvetica**. Click the **Font Size arrow**, and, if necessary, click **11**. Compare your screen with **Figure 2**.
4. Click cell **E4**. In the **Cells group**, click the **Insert button arrow**, and then click **Insert Columns** to insert two blank columns.
5. In cell **E4**, type Grasses and then press Tab. In cell **F4**, type Misc. and then press Tab.

■ **Continue to the next page to complete the skill**

Row 1 selected

Font type and size changed

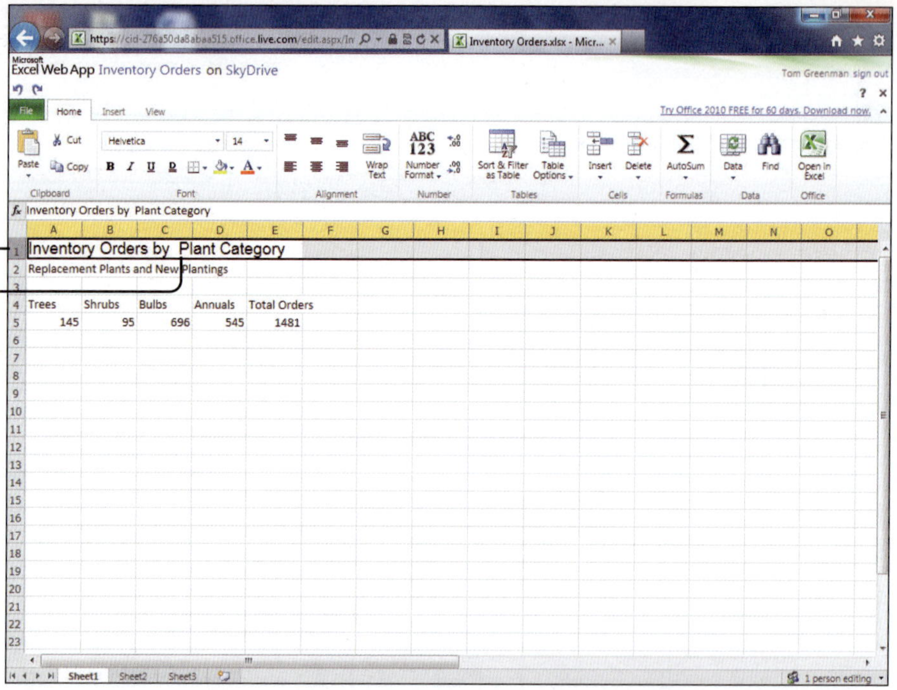

Figure 1

Formatting changed

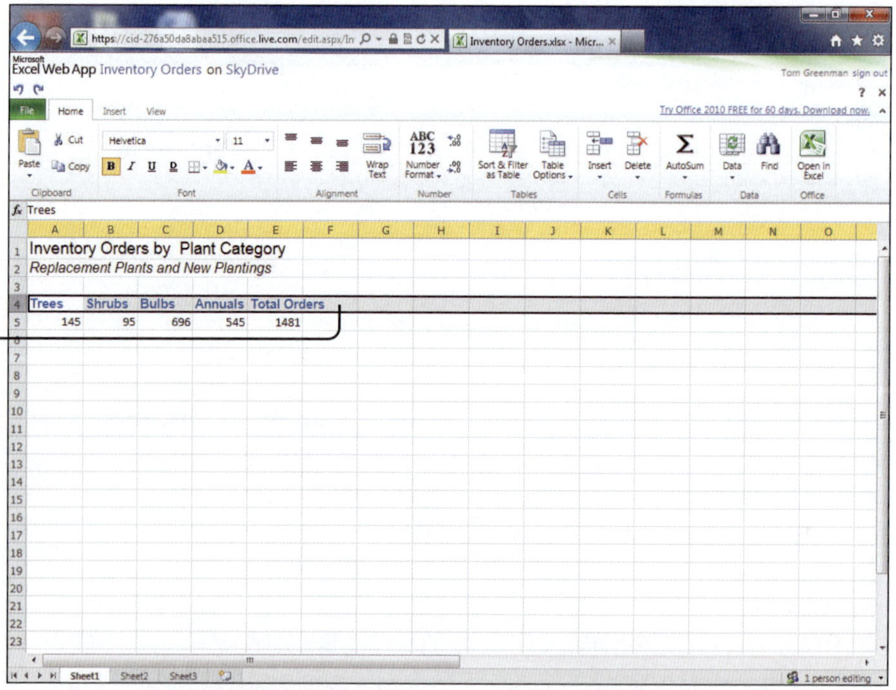

Figure 2

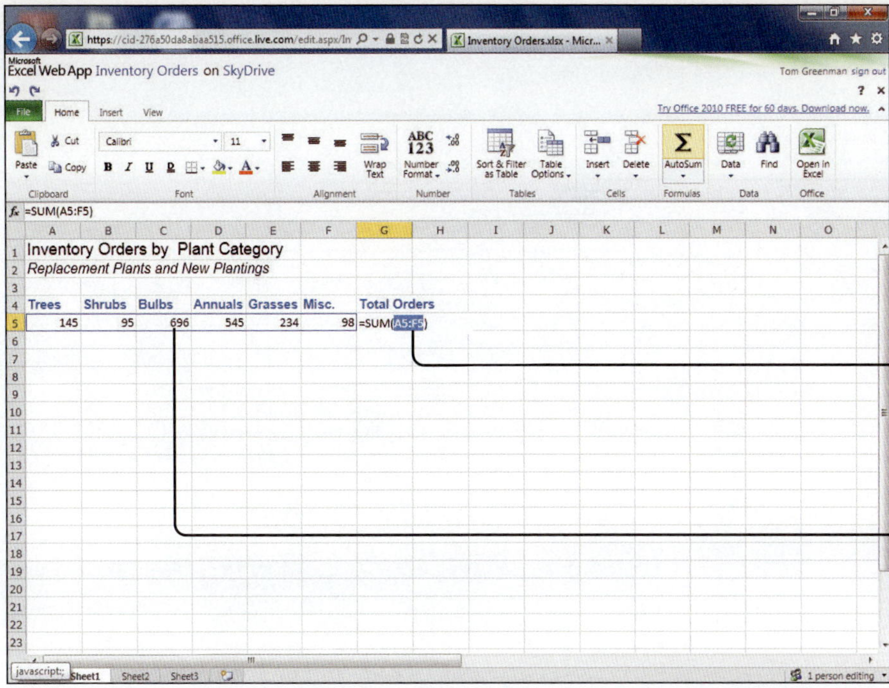

Figure 3

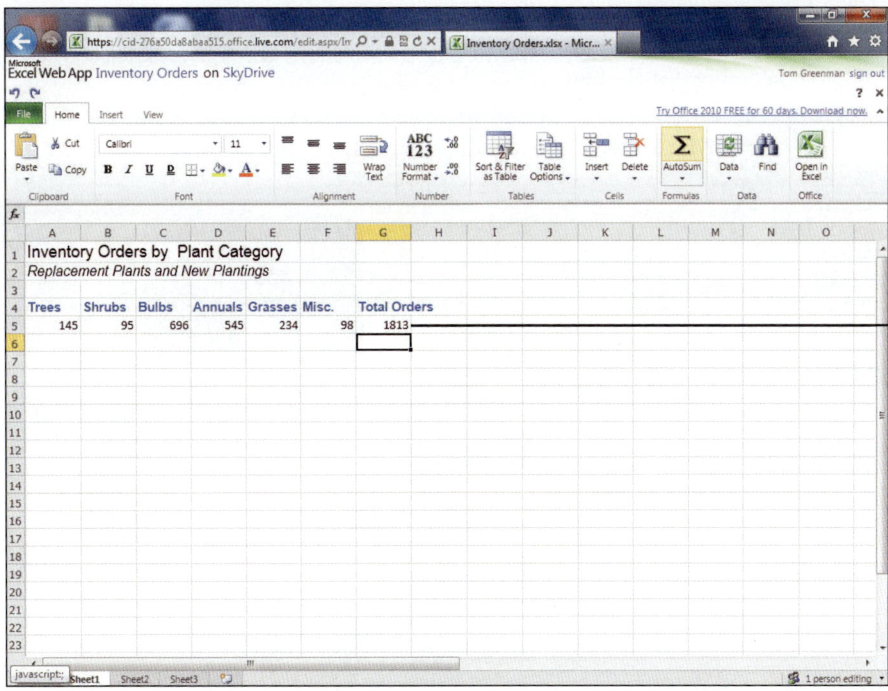

Figure 4

6. In cell **E5**, type 234 and then press Tab. In cell **F5**, type 98 and then press Tab.

   The Total Orders cell value does not update because the cell range in the function argument does not include the new columns.

7. With cell **G5** selected, click the top half of the **AutoSum** button, and then compare your screen with **Figure 3**.

   The cell reference in the Sum function will be updated to A5:F5.

8. Press Enter, and then compare your screen with **Figure 4**.

   The new total has been updated to include all of the columns.

9. Create a **Full-screen snip**. Save the snip in your **Web Apps Chapter 2** folder as Lastname_Firstname_wa02_Gardens_2 **Close** the **Snipping Tool** window. Submit the snip as directed by your instructor.

10. At the top of the screen, click the **SkyDrive** link to return to SkyDrive. Under **Documents**, verify that **Inventory Orders** is listed.

■ **You have completed Skill 5 of 10**

- ▶ ***PowerPoint Web App*** is the part of Office Web Apps used to work with PowerPoint presentations.
- ▶ A ***slide*** is an individual page or screen in a presentation. Slides can contain text, pictures, tables, charts, and other multimedia or graphic objects.
- ▶ You can select a presentation ***theme***—a predefined set of colors, fonts, lines, fill effects, and graphics—that is applied to your entire document, workbook, presentation, or web page.
- ▶ As you develop presentations, you can add new slides by adding various layouts.

1. On the SkyDrive page, in the SkyDrive navigation bar, to the right of *Create*, click **Create PowerPoint presentation**. Compare your screen with **Figure 1**.
2. In the **Name**, type Composting Made Easy and then click the **Create** button.
3. In the **Select Theme** dialog box that displays, scroll to locate and then click **Austin**—the green theme. Click the **Apply** button. If the *Improve Your Experience* information message displays, click the **Close** button [x].
4. Click the **Title** placeholder—the placeholder with the text **Click to add title**—and then type Composting Made Easy Click out of the Title placeholder.
5. Click in the **Subtitle** placeholder, and then type Aspen Falls Parks and Recreation Click outside of the subtitle placeholder. Compare your screen with **Figure 2**.

■ Continue to the next page to complete the skill

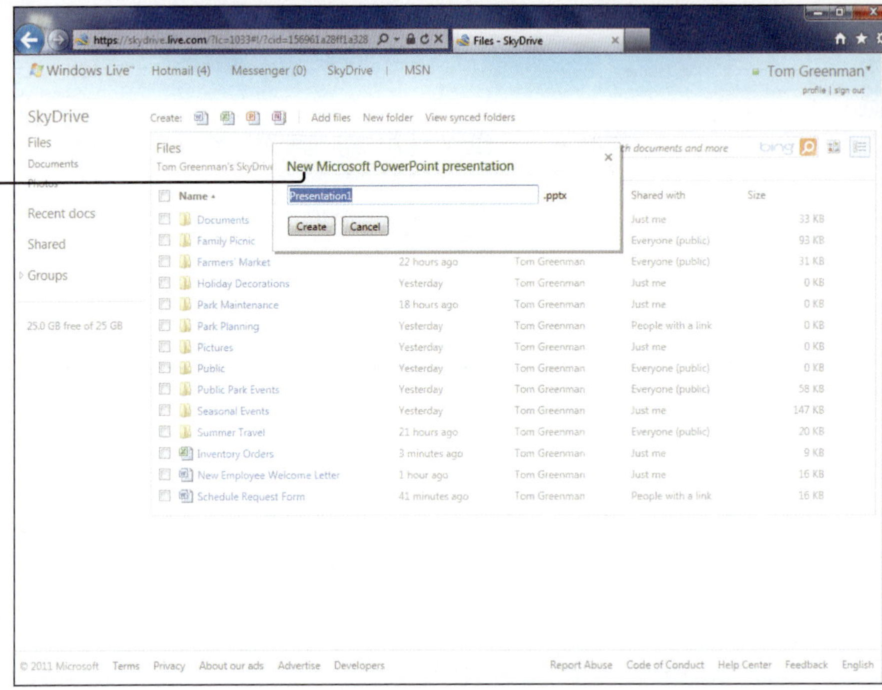

Figure 1

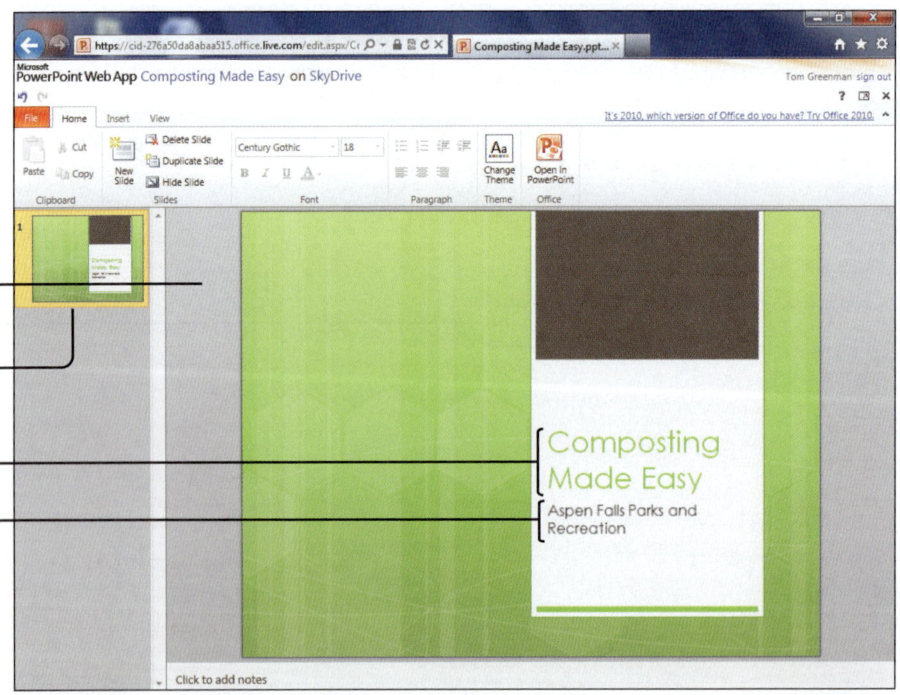

Figure 2

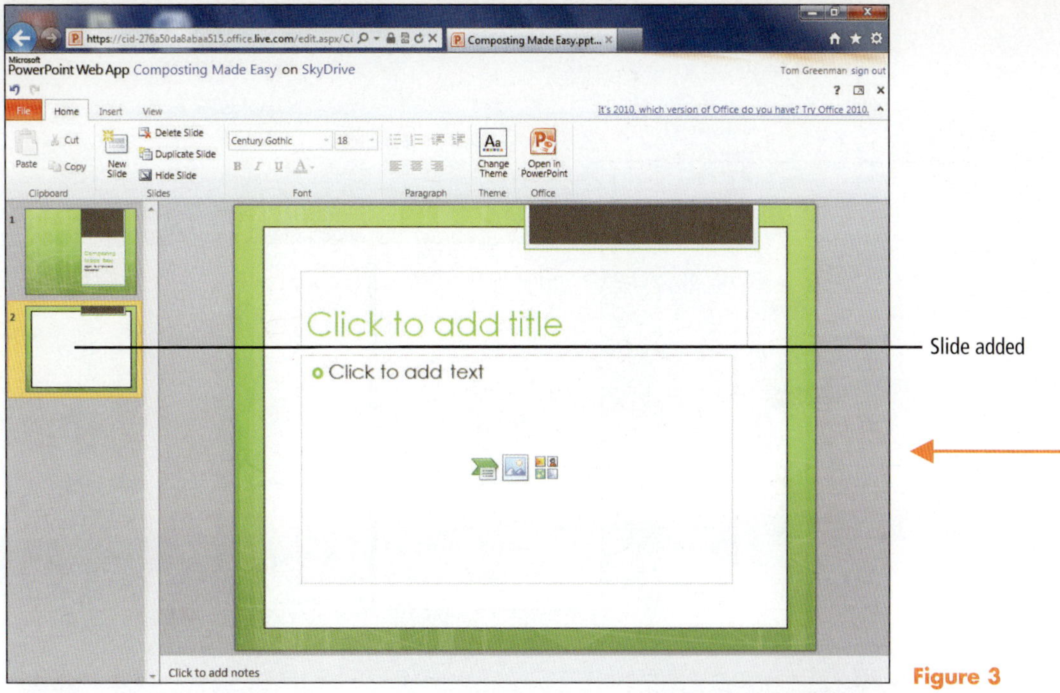

Figure 3

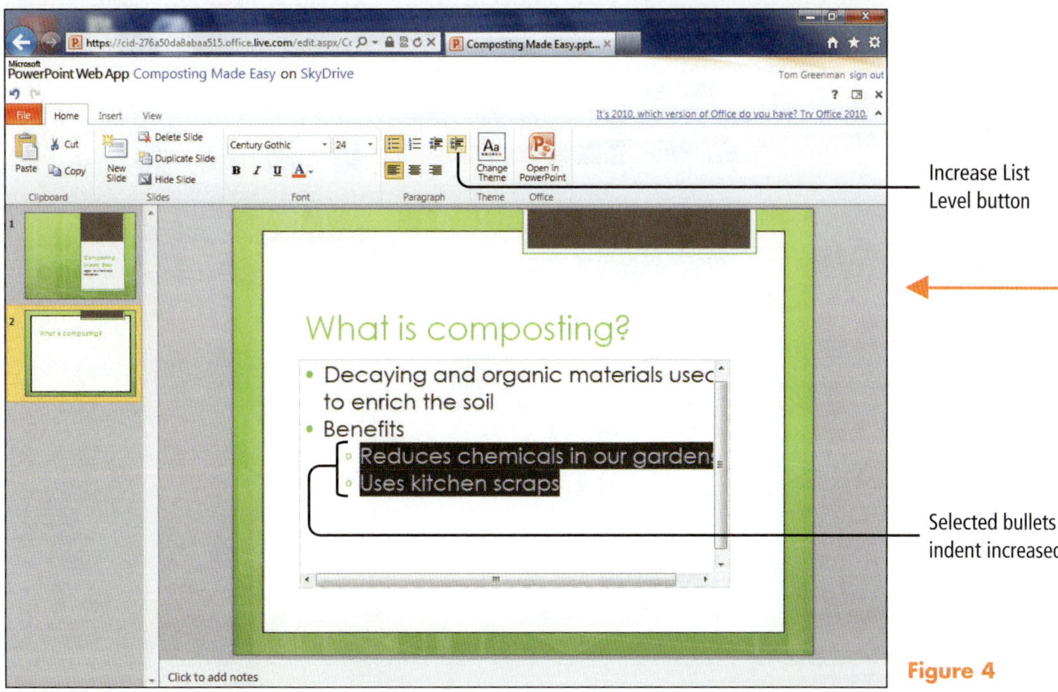

Figure 4

6. On **the Home tab**, in the **Slides group**, click **New Slide**. In the **New Slide** dialog box, click **Title and Content**, and then click the **Add Slide** button. Compare your screen with **Figure 3**.
7. With slide 2 displayed, click in the **Title** placeholder, and then type What is composting?
8. Click in the Content placeholder—the placeholder with the text **Click to add text**—and then type Decaying and organic materials used to enrich the soil
9. Press Enter to add a second bullet, and then type Benefits Press Enter, and then type Reduces chemicals in our gardens Press Enter, and then for the fourth bullet, type Uses kitchen scraps
10. Drag to select the last two bullets. In the **Paragraph group**, click the **Increase List Level** button, and then compare your screen with **Figure 4**.
11. Click outside the placeholder but keep the presentation open for the next skill.

    PowerPoint Web App automatically saves your work. There is no need to click a Save button.

■ **You have completed Skill 6 of 10**

- You can enhance your PowerPoint presentation by adding ***SmartArt graphics***—designer-quality visual representations of information that communicate ideas in a variety of layouts.
- The Slide Show view enables you to preview your presentation as you develop it.

1. With the Composting Made Easy presentation open, in the **Slides group**, click the **New Slide** button. In the **New Slide** dialog box, click the **Content with Caption** thumbnail. Click the **Add Slide** button, and then compare your screen with **Figure 1**.
2. On the right side of slide 3, click the **Title** placeholder, and then type How does composting help our planet? In the **Subtitle** placeholder, type It replenishes soil nutrients.
3. On the left side, in the **Click to add text** box, click the **Insert SmartArt Graphic** button. On the **SmartArt tab**, in the **Layouts group**, click the **More Layouts arrow**, and then click **Multidirectional Cycle**—the third thumbnail in the fourth row. Compare your screen with **Figure 2**.

■ **Continue to the next page to complete the skill**

Newly added slide

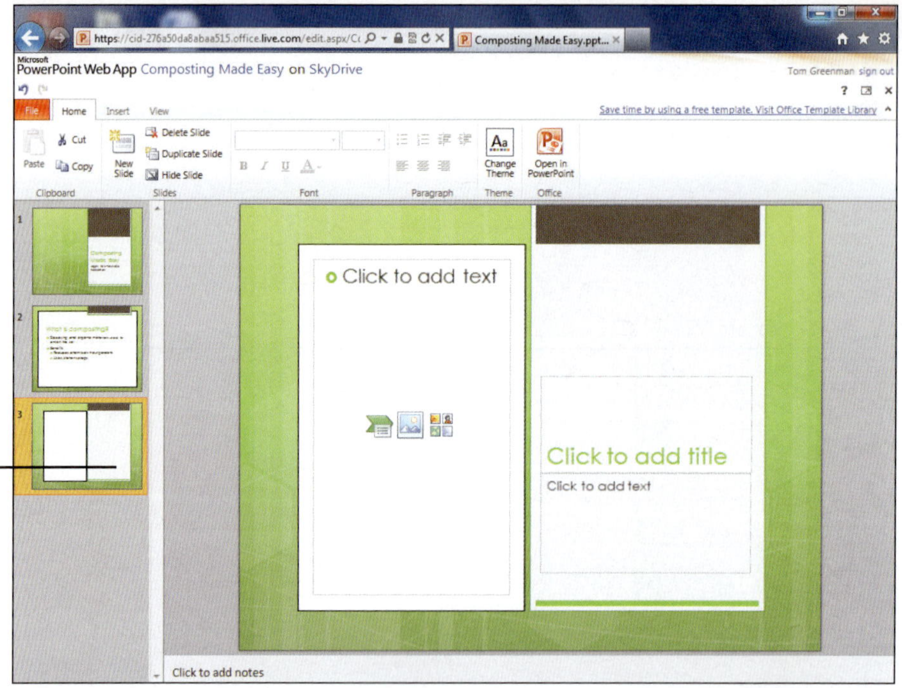

Figure 1

More Layouts arrow

Multidirectional Cycle layout

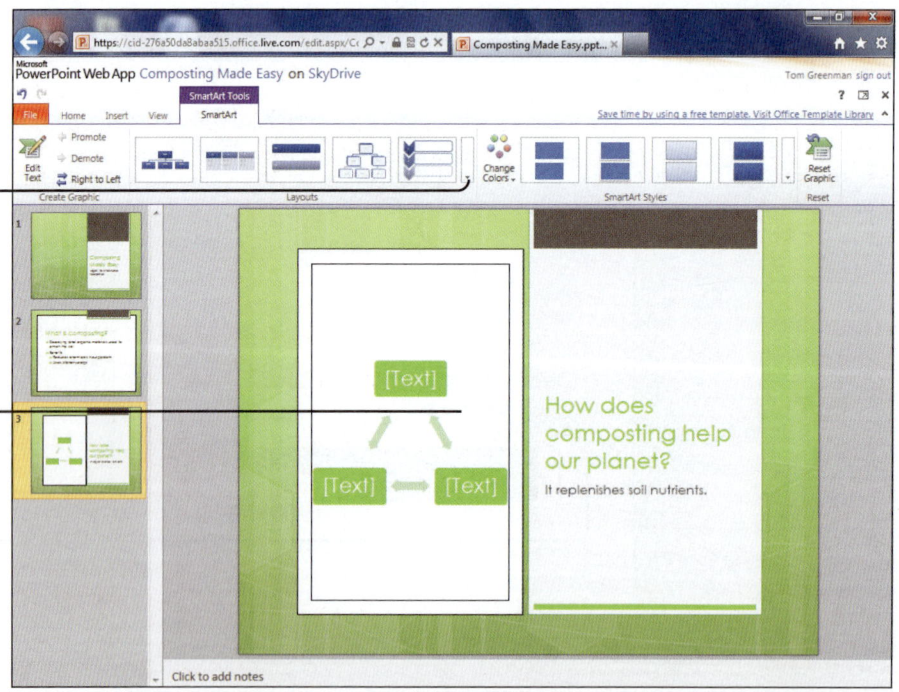

Figure 2

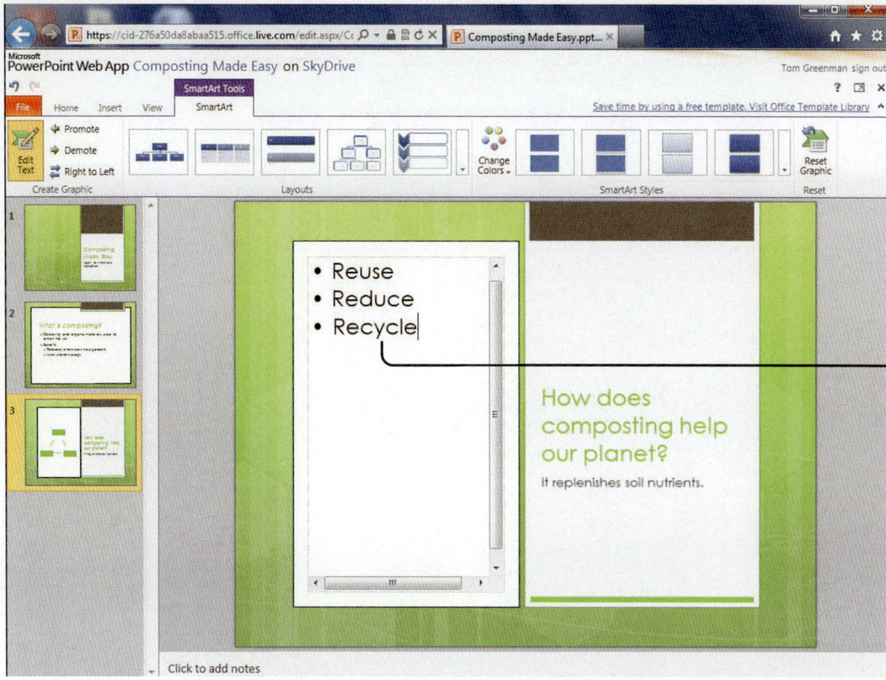

SmartArt graphic

Figure 3

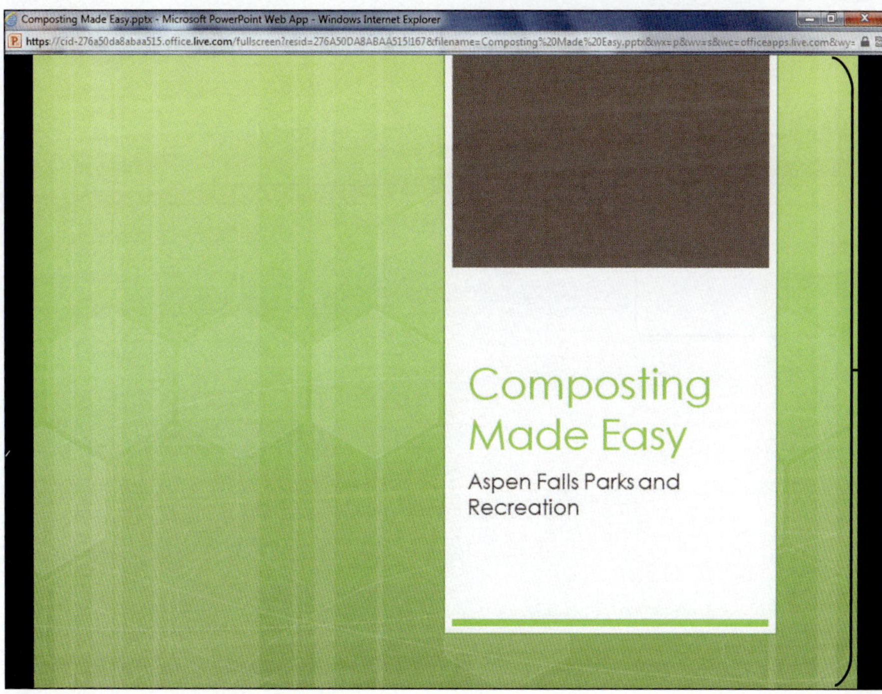

Slide Show view

Figure 4

4. In the **SmartArt graphic**, click the top **Text** placeholder to display three bullets. In the first bullet, type Reuse Click beside the second bullet and type Reduce Click beside the third bullet and type Recycle Compare your screen with **Figure 3**.
5. Click the **View tab**. In the **Presentation Views group**, click **Slide Show** to display the SmartArt text. Click **Slide Show** one more time, and then compare your screen with **Figure 4**.

   You may receive a message about blocked pop-ups. You can Allow once or click Options for this site and then Always allow.

6. Click the left mouse button to move through the slide show. At the end of the slide show, click the left mouse button one more time to exit the slide show.
7. Create a **Full-screen snip**. Save the snip in your **Web Apps Chapter 2** folder as Lastname_Firstname_wa02_Gardens_3 **Close** the **Snipping Tool** window. Submit the snip as directed by your instructor.
8. At the top of the screen, click the **SkyDrive** link to save the presentation and display the SkyDrive page.

- **You have completed Skill 7 of 10**

- ***OneNote Web App*** is the part of Office Web Apps used to manage information such as text, images, and multimedia in one location as if you had a single notebook.
- A OneNote notebook can be shared with others so that they can view and edit the notebook.
- OneNote notebooks are organized into sections and pages.

1. On the SkyDrive page, in the SkyDrive navigation bar, to the right of *Create*, click **Create OneNote notebook**. Compare your screen with **Figure 1**.
2. In the **Name**, type Gardener's Notebook Click the **Create** button. If the *Improve Your Experience* information message displays, click the **Close** button ×. Compare your screen with **Figure 2**.

   The left pane of the notebook—navigation pane—can be organized into sections. Within each section, pages can be added. The right side of the notebook—page pane—displays the page title placeholder at the top. Whatever is typed there will become the page title in the navigation pane.

■ **Continue to the next page to complete the skill**

New Microsoft OneNote notebook page

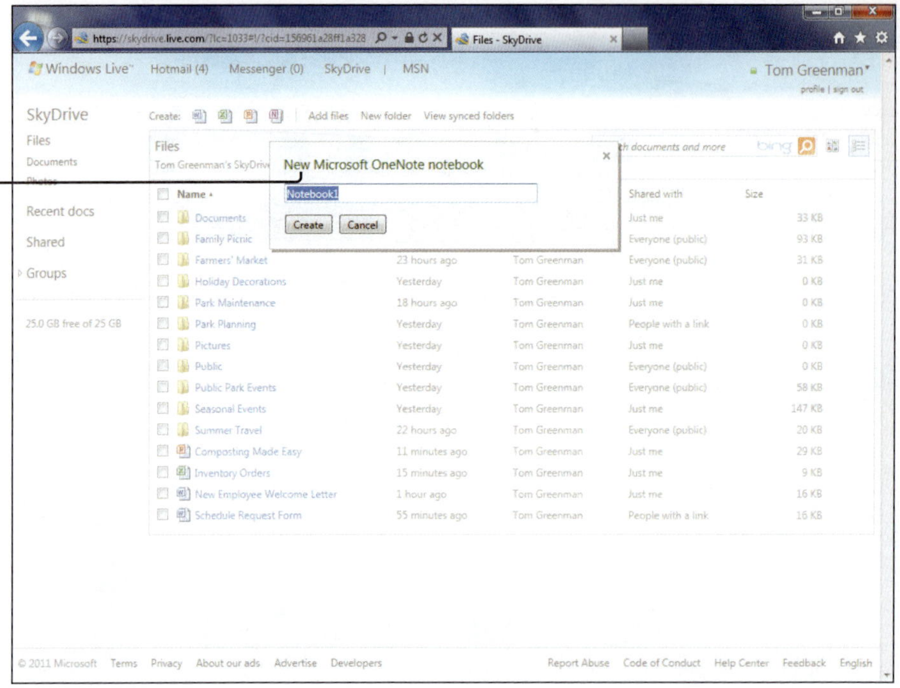

Figure 1

Page pane

Section

Page

Page title placeholder

Navigation pane

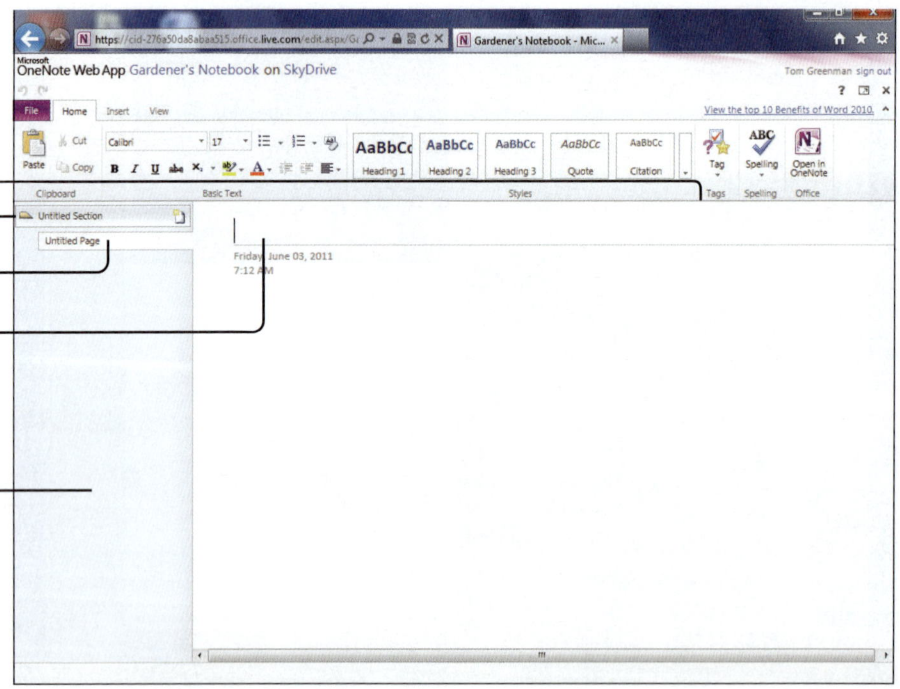

Figure 2

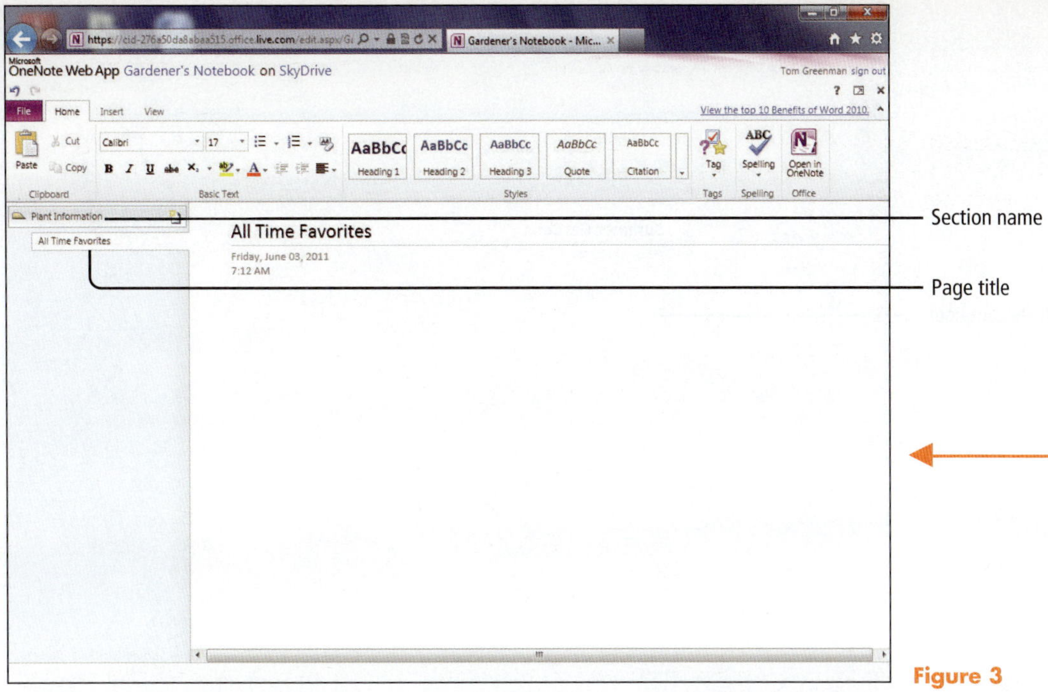

Figure 3

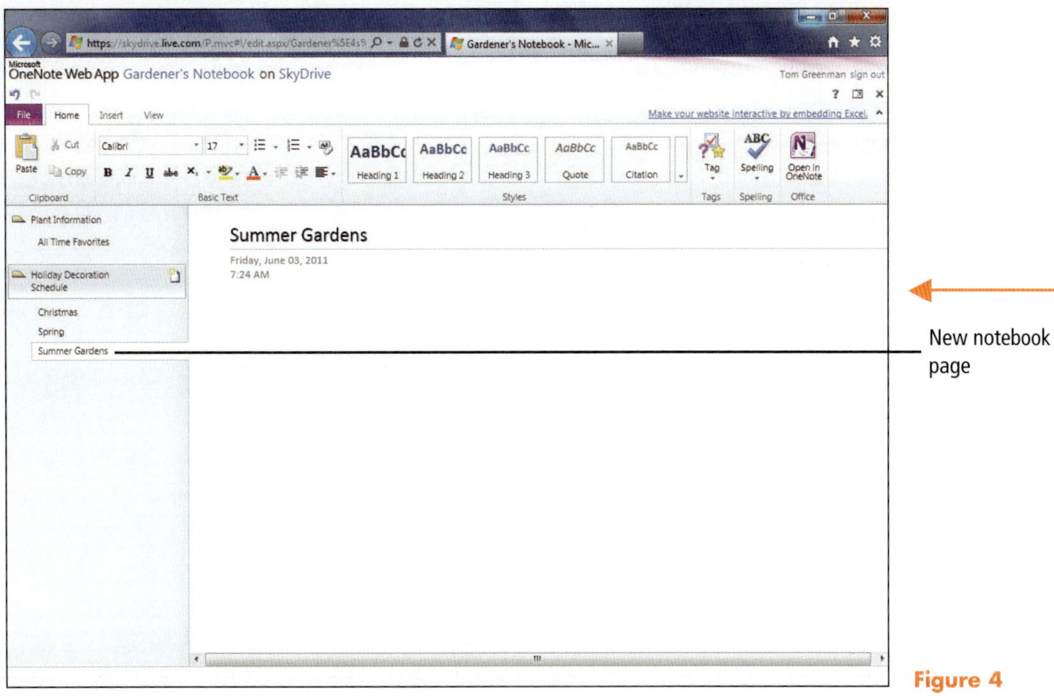

Figure 4

3. With the insertion point in the page title area, type All Time Favorites On the navigation pane, right-click **Untitled Section**, and then click **Rename**. In the **Section Name** dialog box, replace the section name with Plant Information and then click the **OK** button. Compare your screen with **Figure 3**.
4. On the **Insert tab**, in the **Notebook group**, click the **New Section** button. In the **Section Name** dialog box, type Holiday Decoration Schedule and then click the **OK** button.
5. In the page title placeholder, type Christmas
6. On the **Insert tab**, in the **Notebook group**, click **New Page**. In the page title placeholder, type Spring
7. Repeat the technique just practiced to add a page named Summer Gardens and then compare your screen with **Figure 4**. Keep the notebook open for the next skill.

- **You have completed Skill 8 of 10**

- Text, tables and hyperlinks can be added to a OneNote notebook.
- ***Note containers*** are placeholders that hold the content on a OneNote page.
- Permissions can be set so that multiple authors can contribute to a notebook.

1. With the Gardner's Notebook open, on the **Summer Gardens** page, below the page title, point to a blank area below the date and time. Double-click to open a note container. Compare your screen with **Figure 1**.
2. In the **note container**, type Participants may enroll for Aspen Parks and Recreation classes to learn how to design and plant their summer gardens by calling the department office between February 1st and March 31st.

   As you type, note containers change their size and shape to fit the content. Adjust your note container to match the figure.
3. Click the **Home tab**, and then to the right of February 1, drag to select the letters *st*. In the **Basic Text group**, click the **Subscript button arrow** [x₁ button], and then click **Superscript**.
4. After the text *March 31*, select the letters *st*, and then apply **Superscript**.
5. Click to the right of the period to deselect the text, and then compare your screen with **Figure 2**.

■ **Continue to the next page to complete the skill**

Note container

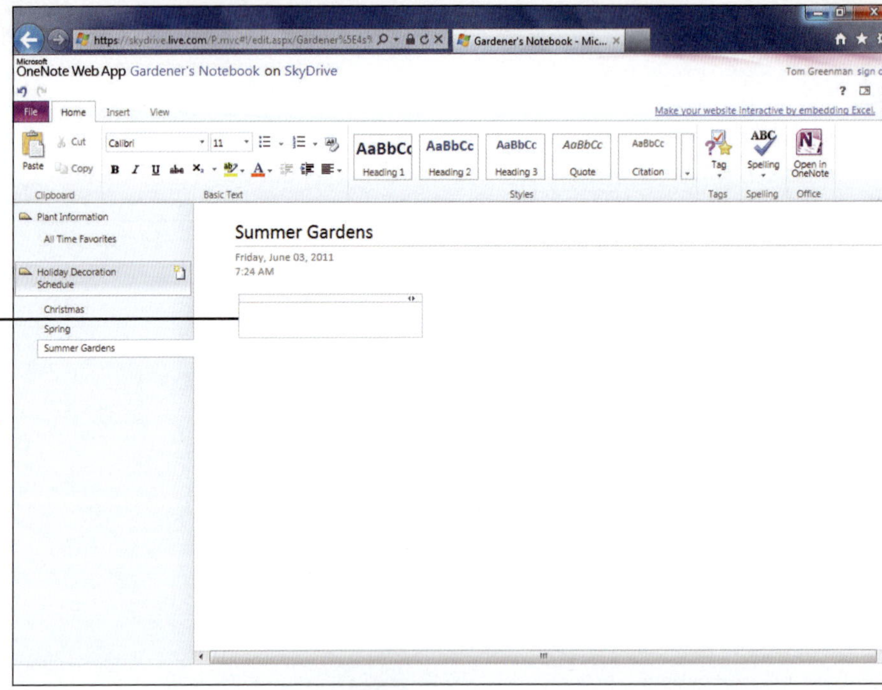

Figure 1

Superscript format applied

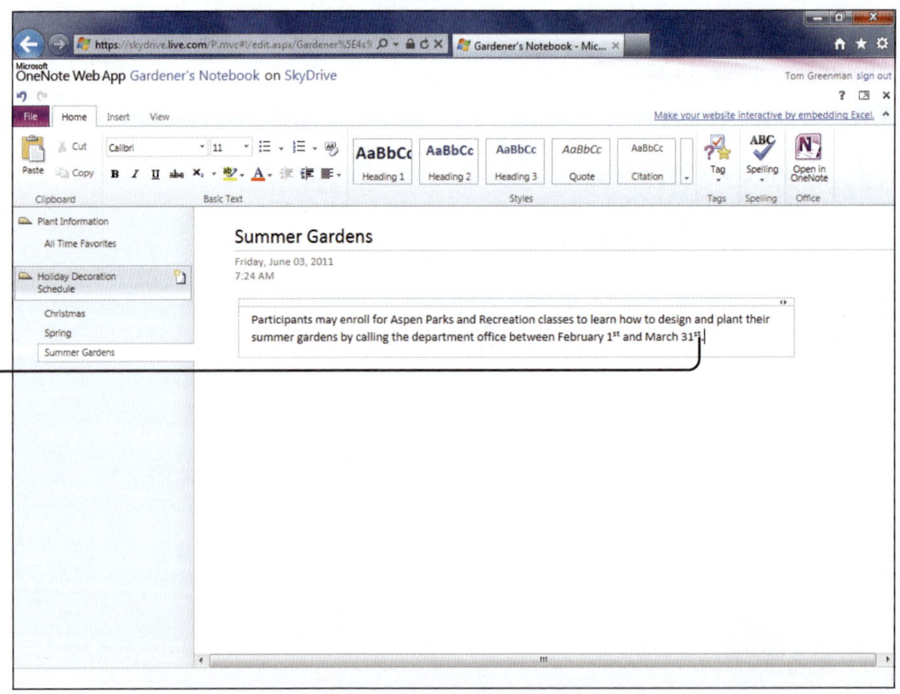

Figure 2

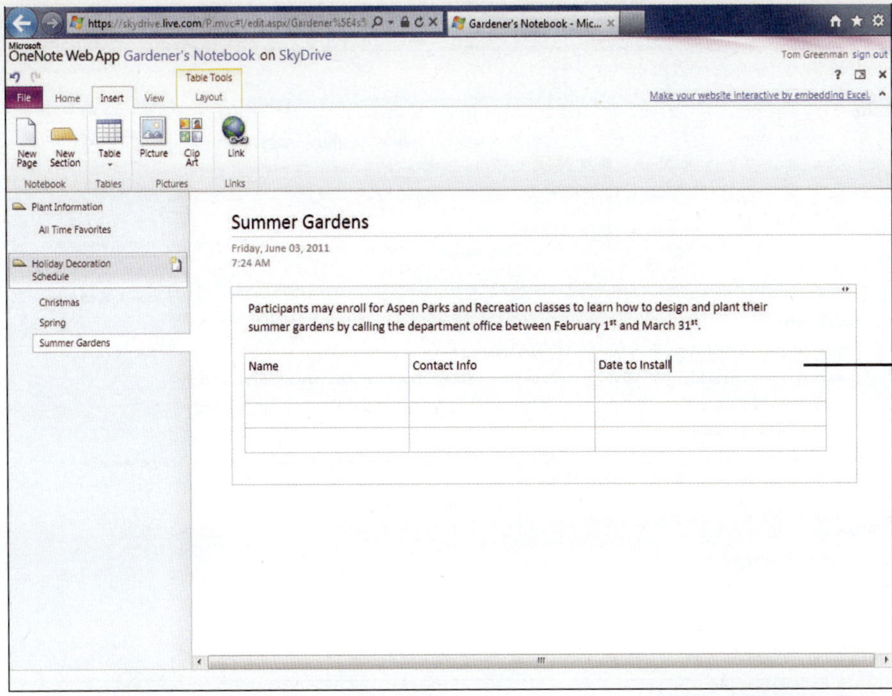

Figure 3

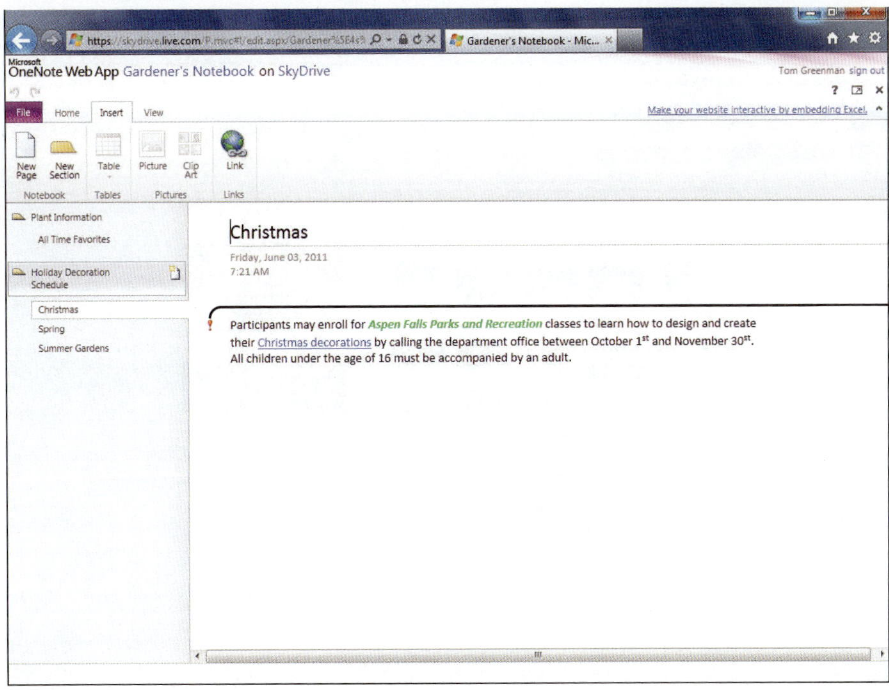

Figure 4

6. Press Enter two times. On the **Insert tab**, click the **Table** button, and then insert a table with 3 columns and 4 rows. In the first cell, type Name Press Tab, and then type Contact Info Press Tab, and then type Date to Install Allow the table to autosize, or if necessary, adjust the columns by dragging the borders. Compare your screen with **Figure 3**.
7. In the navigation pane, click **Christmas**. Click in a blank area below the date and time, and type the text shown in Figure 4.
8. In the text just added, after each date, apply the **Superscript** format as appropriate.
9. Select the text *Christmas decorations*. On the **Insert tab**, in the **Links group**, click **Link**. In the **Link** dialog box, in the **Address** box, type http://www.christmasplace.com and then click the **Insert** button.
10. On the **View tab**, in the **Authors group**, click **Show Authors** to display the author name next to the text. Click **Show Authors** again to toggle the author names off.
11. Select the phrase *Aspen Falls Parks and Recreation*. On the **Home tab**, in the **Basic Text group**, click the **Bold** button, and then click the **Italic** button, click the **Font Color arrow**, and then under **Standard Colors**, click **Dark Green**.
12. In the **Tag group**, click the **Tag** button, and then click **Critical**. Compare your screen with **Figure 4**.
13. Take a **Full-screen snip**. Navigate to your storage device. Name the snip Lastname_Firstname_wa02_Gardens_4 and save it as a JPEG file (*.jpg) in the **Web Apps Chapter 2** folder.

- **You have completed Skill 9 of 10**

- You can use Office Web Apps to insert graphics such as clip art and photos into Office documents.
- You can also resize graphics and add borders or frames for added emphasis.

1. Return to the SkyDrive page and click the **New Employee Welcome Letter** check box. Then click **Edit in Browser**. Compare your screen with **Figure 1**.
2. At the top of the page in the address, make sure the insertion point is to the left of *Aspen Falls Parks and Recreation Department*. On the **Insert tab**, in the **Pictures group**, click the **Clip Art** button.
3. In the **Insert Clip Art** dialog box, in the **Search** box, type Gardens and click the **Search** button.
4. Scroll down to locate the picture of hands holding some seeds, and then click the picture to display information about the clip. If that clip is not available, click a similar graphic. Compare your screen with **Figure 2**.

■ **Continue to the next page to complete the skill**

New Employee Welcome Letter

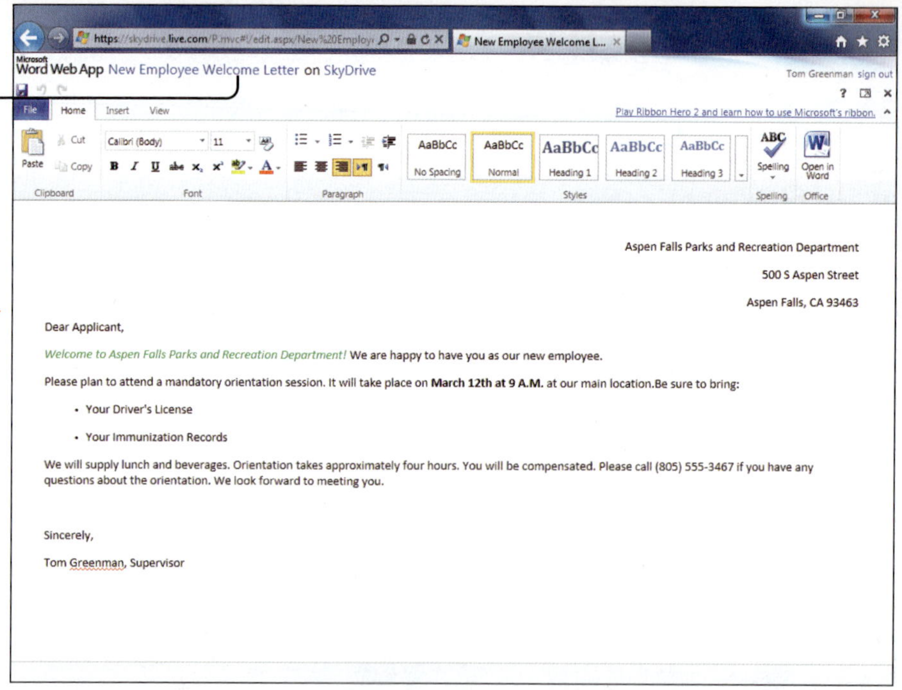

Figure 1

Details about selected clip (Yours may vary)

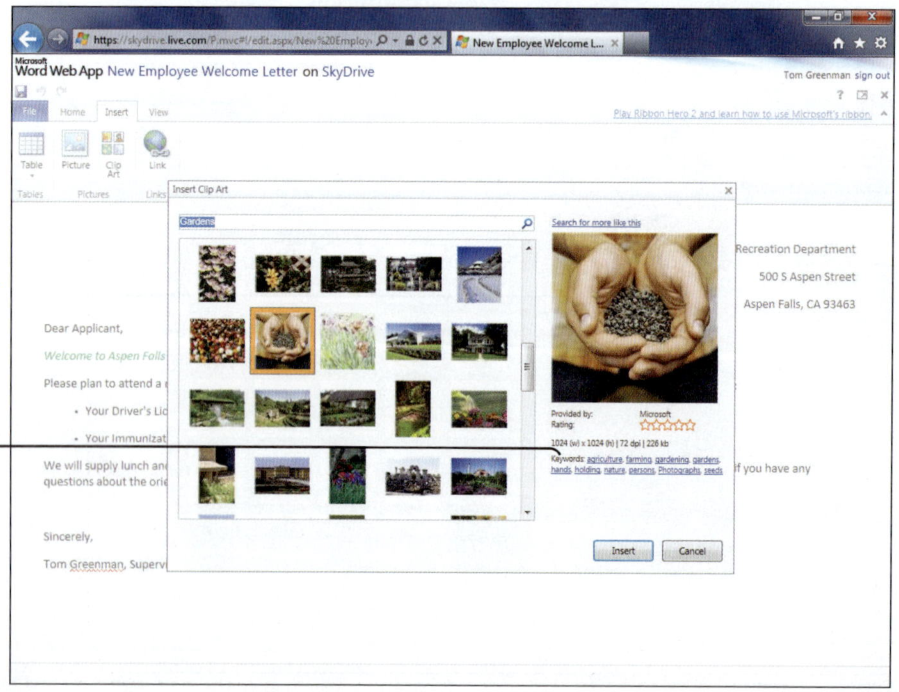

Figure 2

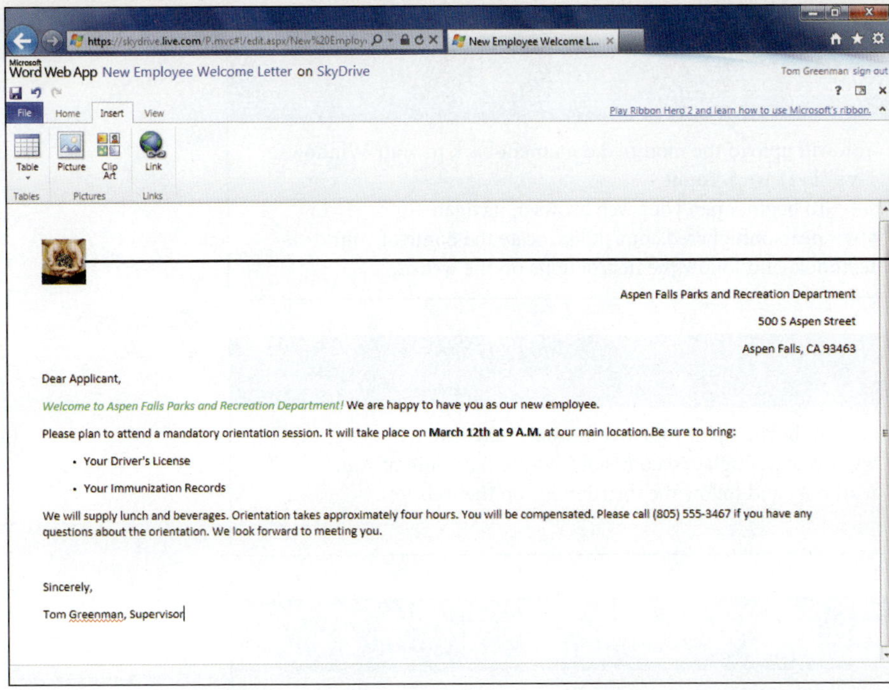

Figure 3

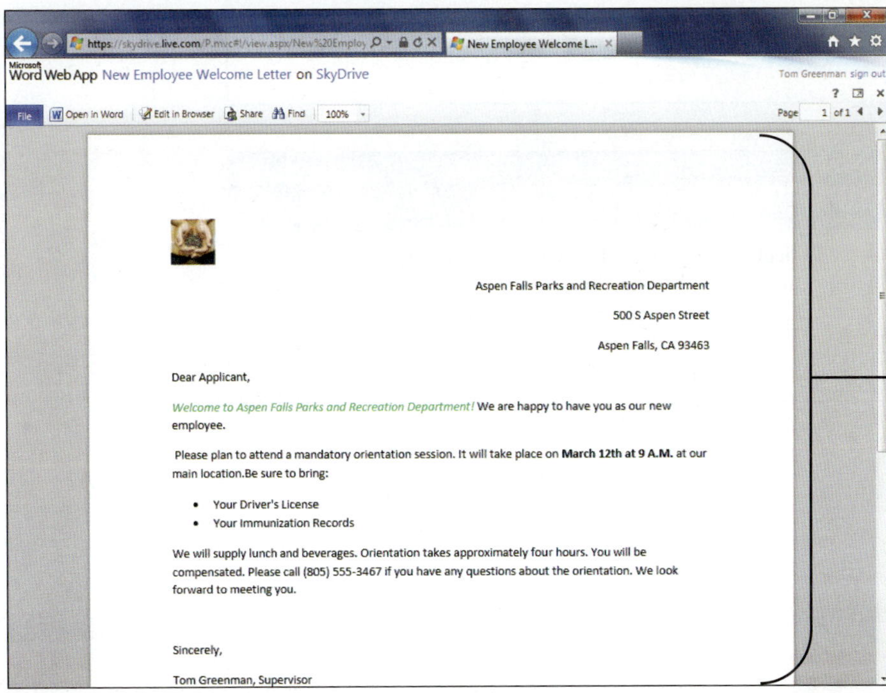

Figure 4

5. In the **Insert Clip Art** dialog box, click the **Insert** button. Wait a few moments for the picture to be inserted, and then click the picture to select it.
6. On the **Format tab**, in the **Image Size group**, click in the **Scale** box, and then type 5% Click to the left of the word *Aspen*, and then click **Save** . Deselect the picture, and then compare your screen with **Figure 3**.
7. On the **View tab**, in the **Document Views group**, click the **Reading View** button. Compare your screen to **Figure 4**.
8. Create a **Full-screen snip**. Save the snip in your Web Apps 2 folder as Lastname_Firstname_wa02_Gardens_5 **Close** **Snipping Tool** window. Submit the snip as directed by your instructor.
9. Click **SkyDrive**, sign out of **Windows Live**, and then click **Close** to close the browser window. Print or submit the snips as directed by your instructor.

Done! You have completed Skill 10 of 10

The following More Skills are located at **www.pearsonhighered.com/skills**

More Skills 11 Edit Files Stored in SkyDrive in Word

If you have Microsoft Office 2010 programs installed on your computer, you can modify documents and files created in Office Web Apps on your computer instead of Office Web Apps.

In More Skills 11, you will download a document from your Windows Live SkyDrive account and modify it using Word 2010. You will upload the modified document back to your Windows Live SkyDrive account.

To begin, open your web browser, navigate to www.pearsonhighered.com/skills, locate the name of your textbook, and follow the instructions on the website.

More Skills 12 Create Excel Web App Charts

You can use Excel Web App to create worksheets that contain charts to visually represent data. In More Skills 12, you will create a worksheet, and then select a range of cells. With the range selected, you will create an Exploded Pie chart.

To begin, open your web browser, navigate to www.pearsonhighered.com/skills, locate the name of your textbook, and follow the instructions on the website.

More Skills 13 Insert Graphics in OneNote Web App Notebooks

Inserting clip art into a notebook is similar to inserting clip art into any Office Web Apps program.

In More Skills 13, you will search for clip art using a specific key term. You will insert the clip art into the notebook.

To begin, open your web browser, navigate to www.pearsonhighered.com/skills, locate the name of your textbook, and follow the instructions on the website.

More Skills 14 Download SkyDrive Files to Your Computer

Documents and files created in Office Web Apps can be downloaded and saved. In More Skills 14, you create a document using Word Web App and save it in your Windows Live SkyDrive account. You will download the document to your computer or storage device.

To begin, open your web browser, navigate to www.pearsonhighered.com/skills, locate the name of your textbook, and follow the instructions on the website.

Key Terms

Online Help Skills

1. Open you browser to start **Internet Explorer.** In the address bar, type office.microsoft.com/en-us/web-apps and then press Enter to display the home page for Microsoft Office Web Apps. Compare your screen with **Figure 1**.
2. Scroll down the page to display **Help with Web Apps**, and then click the **Embed a presentation on a webpage** link.
3. Read the article, and then answer the following question: When might you want to embed a presentation on a web page?

Figure 1

Matching

Match each term in the second column with its correct definition in the first column by writing the letter of the term on the blank line in front of the correct definition.

___ **1.** The part of Office Web Apps used to create workbooks and worksheets.

___ **2.** An Excel feature that inserts prewritten functions into a cell.

___ **3.** The part of Office Web Apps used to manage information such as text, images, and multimedia in one location as if you had a single notebook.

___ **4.** Designer-quality visual representations of information that communicate ideas in a variety of layouts.

___ **5.** An Excel file that contains one or more worksheets.

___ **6.** The location of a specific cell or range in a spreadsheet.

___ **7.** A predefined set of colors, fonts, lines, and fill effects that look good together and can be applied to your entire document or presentation.

___ **8.** Web-based versions of Microsoft Office programs—Word, Excel, PowerPoint, and OneNote—that are available online through Windows Live.

___ **9.** An individual page in a presentation that can contain text, pictures, tables, charts, and other multimedia or graphic objects.

___ **10.** A process that performs mathematical functions according to cell references and the values in their parentheses.

A AutoSum

B Cell reference

C Excel Web App

D Function

E Office Web Apps

F OneNote Web App

G Slide

H SmartArt graphics

I Theme

J Workbook

Multiple Choice

Choose the correct answer.

1. Office Web Apps files are saved directly ___.
   - A. at your Hotmail address
   - B. in your Windows Live SkyDrive account
   - C. on your school's network
2. The intersection of one column and one row in an Excel worksheet is called a ___.
   - A. value
   - B. slide
   - C. cell
3. The data in a cell is called its ___.
   - A. theme
   - B. function
   - C. value
4. A placeholder used to hold the content on a OneNote page is called a ___.
   - A. note container
   - B. slide
   - C. cell reference
5. The part of Office Web Apps used to create slides and presentations is called ___.
   - A. Word Web App
   - B. PowerPoint Web App
   - C. OneNote Web App
6. The ___ feature is helpful to identify who contributed which content in a notebook.
   - A. Show Authors
   - B. Display Authors
   - C. Show Contributors
7. A cell's ___ can be modified by font type, size and color.
   - A. function
   - B. theme
   - C. format
8. The part of Office Web Apps used to create documents such as letters, forms, and reports is called ___.
   - A. Word Web App
   - B. OneNote Web App
   - C. PowerPoint Web App
9. A ___ is used in Excel to store and work with data.
   - A. slide
   - B. worksheet
   - C. note container
10. Office Web Apps files can be shared by setting ___.
    - A. Windows Live
    - B. Hotmail
    - C. permissions

Topics for Discussion

1. In this chapter, you practiced using the Show Authors feature in OneNote Web App. How can this feature be used? In what ways would you use it for school? For work?
2. In this chapter, you learned that Office Web Apps can be accessed from any Internet-connected computer. What are the benefits of this feature?

Skill Check

To complete this project, you will need the following files:

- **New blank Office Web App documents**

You will save your snips as:

- **Lastname_Firstname_wa02_Recycle_1**
- **Lastname_Firstname_wa02_Recycle_2**
- **Lastname_Firstname_wa02_Recycle_3**
- **Lastname_Firstname_wa02_Recycle_4**

1. Sign in to Windows Live. Point to **SkyDrive**, and then click **New Word document**.
2. In the **Name**, type Spring Fling Recycling and then click the **Create** button.
3. In the new document, type Spring Fling Recycling Event and press Enter. Type March 3rd Select **rd**, and then click **Superscript**. Click to the right of **rd** to deselect it. Press Enter, and then type 9 A.M.-3 P.M. Press Enter, and then type City Hall Parking Lot
4. Press Enter two times, and then on the **Insert tab**, click the **Clip Art** button.
5. Search for Recycling Click the picture of the Earth inside a recycling symbol or a similar picture, and then click the **Insert** button.
6. Select all the text. On the **Home tab**, change the font to **Arial** and the font size to **18**. Click to deselect the text, and then compare your screen to **Figure 1**.
7. Create a **Full-screen snip**. Save the snip in your **Web Apps Chapter 2** folder as Lastname_Firstname_wa02_Recycle_1 **Close** the **Snipping Tool** window. Submit the snip as directed by your instructor.
8. Click **Save**, and then click the **SkyDrive** link.
9. On the SkyDrive navigation bar, click **Create Excel workbook**. Name the file Recycling Data and then click the **Create** button.
10. In cell **A1**, type Recycling Data by Category In cell **A2**, type Glass Continue down column A, typing Metal and then Newspaper In cell **A5**, type Total Adjust columns if needed so that the word *Newspaper* fits in one cell. In cell **B2**, type 9500 In cell **B3**, type 9760 In cell **B4**, type 9878
11. Click cell **B5**, click the top half of the **AutoSum** button, and then press Enter. Compare your screen with **Figure 2**.

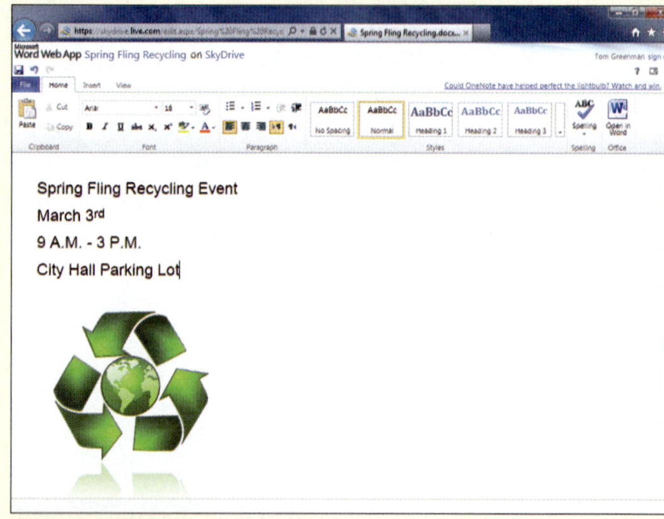

Figure 1

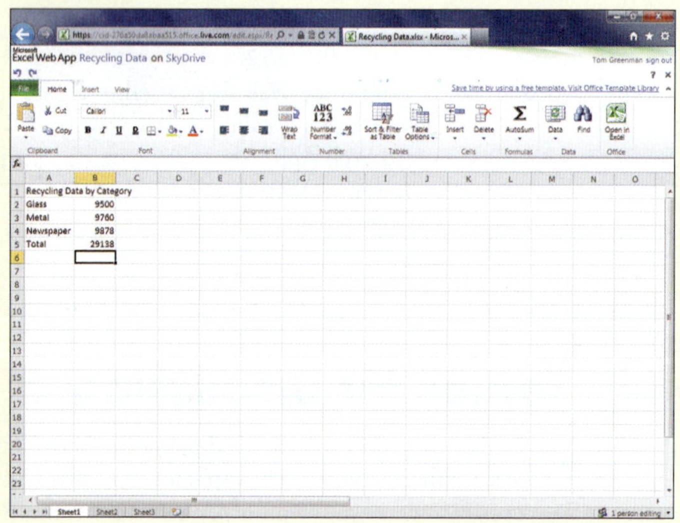

Figure 2

■ Continue to the next page to complete this Skill Check

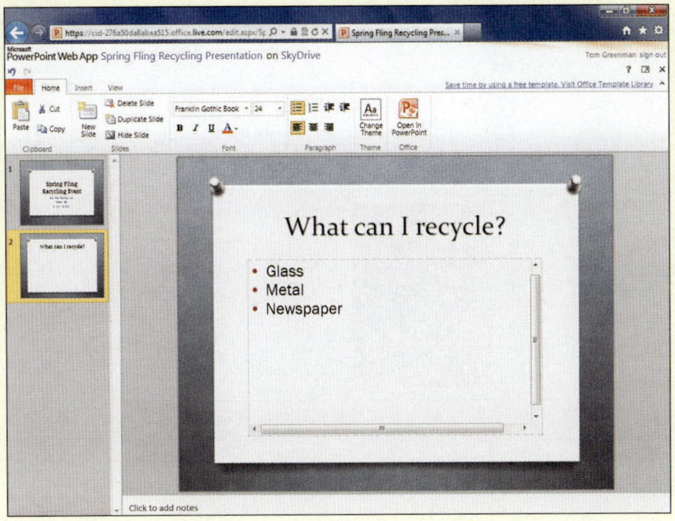

Figure 3

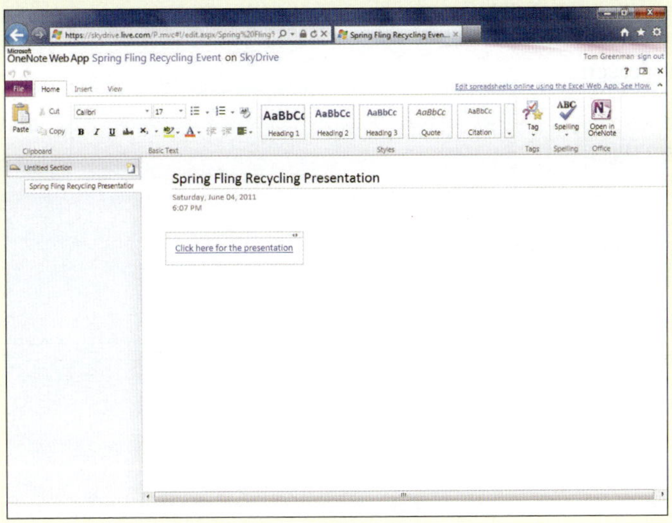

Figure 4

12. Create a **Full-screen** snip. Save the snip in your **Web Apps Chapter 2** folder as Lastname_Firstname_wa02_Recycle_2 **Close** the **Snipping Tool** window. Submit the snip as directed by your instructor.

13. Click the **SkyDrive** link. Create **PowerPoint presentation**. Type Spring Fling Recycling Presentation and then click the **Create** button.

14. In the Select Theme dialog box, apply the **Pushpin** theme.

15. In the **Title** placeholder, type Spring Fling Recycling Event In the **Subtitle** placeholder, type City Hall Parking Lot Press Enter, and then type March 3rd Press Enter, and then type 9 A.M.-3 P.M. Click outside of the Subtitle placeholder.

16. In the **Slides group**, click **New Slide**, click **Title and Content**, and then click **Add Slide**. Add the title What can I recycle? In the Content placeholder, type Glass and then press Enter. Type Metal and then press Enter. Type Newspaper and then compare your screen with **Figure 3**.

17. Click the Title slide. Create a **Full-screen snip**. Save the snip in your **Web Apps Chapter 2** folder as Lastname_Firstname_wa02_Recycle_3 **Close** the **Snipping Tool** window. Submit the snip as directed by your instructor.

18. Click the **SkyDrive** link, click **Create OneNote notebook**.

19. In the **Name**, type Spring Fling Recycling Event and then click the **Create** button.

20. Type Spring Fling Recycling Presentation Under the date and time, double-click, and then in the note container, type Click here for the presentation

21. Click the **SkyDrive** link. Click the **Spring Fling Recycling Presentation** check box. On the right, under **Sharing** click **Share**. Then click **Get a link** on the left.

22. On the **Get a link** dialog box, under **View only**, click **Get a link**. Right-click the link and click **Copy**. Close the dialog box.

23. Click the **Spring Fling Recycling Event** check box, and then click **Edit** in Browser. In the note container, select the phrase **Click here for the presentation**.

24. On the **Insert tab**, in the **Links group**, click the **Link** button. Click in the **Address** box, and then press Ctrl + V to paste the presentation link. Click **Insert**, and then compare your screen with **Figure 4**.

25. Create a **Full-screen snip**. Save the snip in your **Web Apps Chapter 2** folder as Lastname_Firstname_wa02_Recycle_4 **Close** the **Snipping Tool** window. Submit the snip as directed by your instructor.

26. Click the **SkyDrive** link. Sign out of **Windows Live**. **Close** the browser, and then print or submit the snips as directed by your instructor.

Done! You have completed the Skill Check

Assess Your Skills 1

To complete this project, you will need the following files:

- **New blank Office Web Apps documents**

You will save your snips as:

- **Lastname_Firstname_wa02_Tourism_1**
- **Lastname_Firstname_wa02_Tourism_2**

1. Sign in to your Windows Live account, navigate to the **SkyDrive** page, and then create a new Word document named Tourism Goals
2. In the new document, type Tourism Goals and then press Enter. Type Bring added income to city merchants and then press Enter. Type Attract new business to the area and then press Enter.
3. **Center align** all of the text. Select **Tourism Goals**, change the font to **Helvetica**, change the font size to **18**, and then apply **Bold**. Select the last two lines, and then change the font size to **14**. After the change is made, deselect the last two lines.
4. With the insertion point at the end of the text, press Enter two times. Search for clip art using the term *Tourism* and insert an appropriate picture, such as Compass west.
5. Reduce the picture's scale to **37.7%**. Deselect the picture and then **Save** the document. Compare your screen with **Figure 1**.
6. Create a **Full-screen snip**. Save the snip in your **Web Apps Chapter 2** folder as Lastname_Firstname_wa02_Tourism_1 **Close** the **Snipping Tool** window. Submit the snip as directed by your instructor.
7. Return to **SkyDrive**. Create a new Excel workbook named Tourism Data
8. In cell **A1**, type Tourism Data and then change the font size to **14** and apply **Bold**.
9. In cell **A2**, type In-State Visitors and in cell A3, type Out-of-State Visitors In cell **A4**, type Total If necessary, adjust columns so that all text is visible.
10. In cell **B2**, type 12200 and in cell **B3**, type 11580
11. In cell **B4**, insert a function that calculates the total of B2 and B3. Compare your screen with **Figure 2**.
12. Create a **Full-screen snip**. Save the snip in your **Web Apps Chapter 2** folder as Lastname_Firstname_wa02_Tourism_2 **Close** the **Snipping Tool** window. Submit the snip as directed by your instructor.
13. Return to **SkyDrive**. Sign out of **Windows Live. Close** the browser, and then print or submit the snips as directed by your instructor.

Done! You have completed Assess Your Skills 1

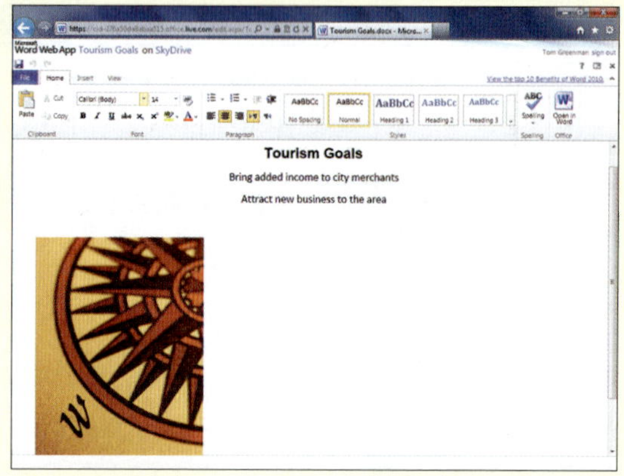

Figure 1

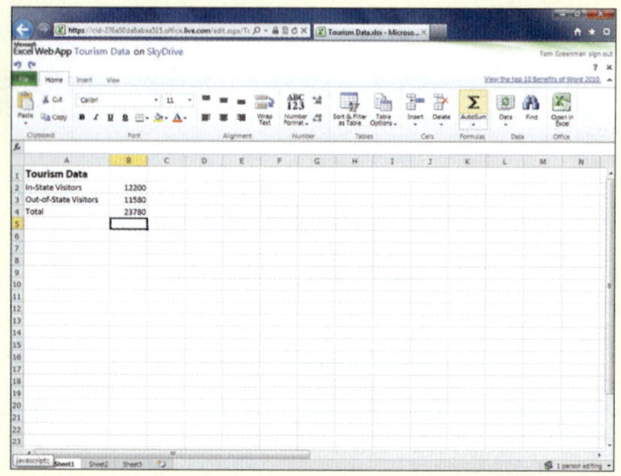

Figure 2

Assess Your Skills 2

Figure 1

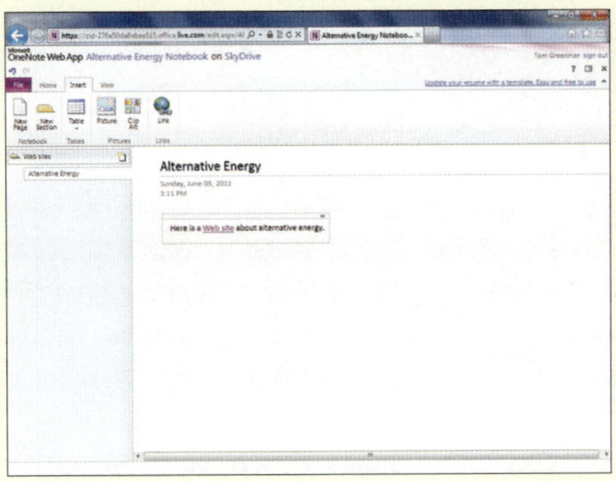

Figure 2

To complete this project, you will need the following files:

- **New blank Office Apps documents**

You will save your snips as:

- **Lastname_Firstname_wa02_Energy_1**
- **Lastname_Firstname_wa02_Energy_2**

1. Sign in to your Windows Live account, navigate to the **SkyDrive** page, and then create a new PowerPoint presentation named Alternative Energy Apply the **Paper** theme.
2. On slide 1, add Alternative Energy as the title and Options for the future as the subtitle.
3. Add a new slide with the **Picture with Caption** layout. Add Wind Energy as the title, and We can use wind to generate electricity. as the content.
4. Select the **Picture** placeholder, and then search for clip art using the term *Windmill.* Insert a picture of a modern windmill. Resize it to match the figure. Compare your screen with **Figure 1**.
5. Create a **Full-screen snip**. Save the snip in your **Web Apps Chapter 2** folder as Lastname_Firstname_wa02_Energy_1 **Close** the **Snipping Tool** window. Submit the snip as directed by your instructor.
6. Return to **SkyDrive**. Create a new **OneNote notebook** named Alternative Energy Notebook
7. Add Alternative Energy as the page title. In a note container, type Here is a Web site about alternative energy Make the word *Web site* a hyperlink to http://www.eere.energy.gov
8. Rename **Untitled Section** to Web sites and then compare your screen with **Figure 2**.
9. Create a **Full-screen snip**. Save the snip in your **Web Apps Chapter 2** folder as Lastname_Firstname_wa02_Energy_2 **Close** the **Snipping Tool** window. Submit the snip as directed by your instructor.
10. Return to **SkyDrive**. Sign out of **Windows Live**. **Close** the browser, and then print or submit the snips as directed by your instructor.

Done! You have completed Assess Your Skills 2

Assess Your Skills Visually

To complete this project, you will need the following file:

- **New blank PowerPoint Web Apps presentation**

You will save your snip as:

- **Lastname_Firstname_wa02_Urban**

Start a new blank presentation, and name the presentation Urban Gardening Presentation Apply the **Summer** theme. Add the title Urban Gardening Add the subtitle Grow Vegetables in Your Own Backyard Create a second slide and add the title What do the plants use to grow? to the slide. Add a subtitle, Use containers to hold each plant and to supply soil for the plant Insert clip art on slide **2**. Add the border **Compound Frame, Black** to the clip art. Create a third slide, as shown in **Figure 1**. Change the subtitle text to font size **20** and add SmartArt graphics.

Compare your screen with **Figure 1**, and then create a **Full-screen snip**. Save the snip in your **Web Apps Chapter 2** folder as Lastname_Firstname_wa02_Urban **Close** the **Snipping Tool** window. Submit the snip as directed by your instructor. Return to **SkyDrive** and sign out of **Windows Live.**

Done! You have completed Assess Your Skills Visually

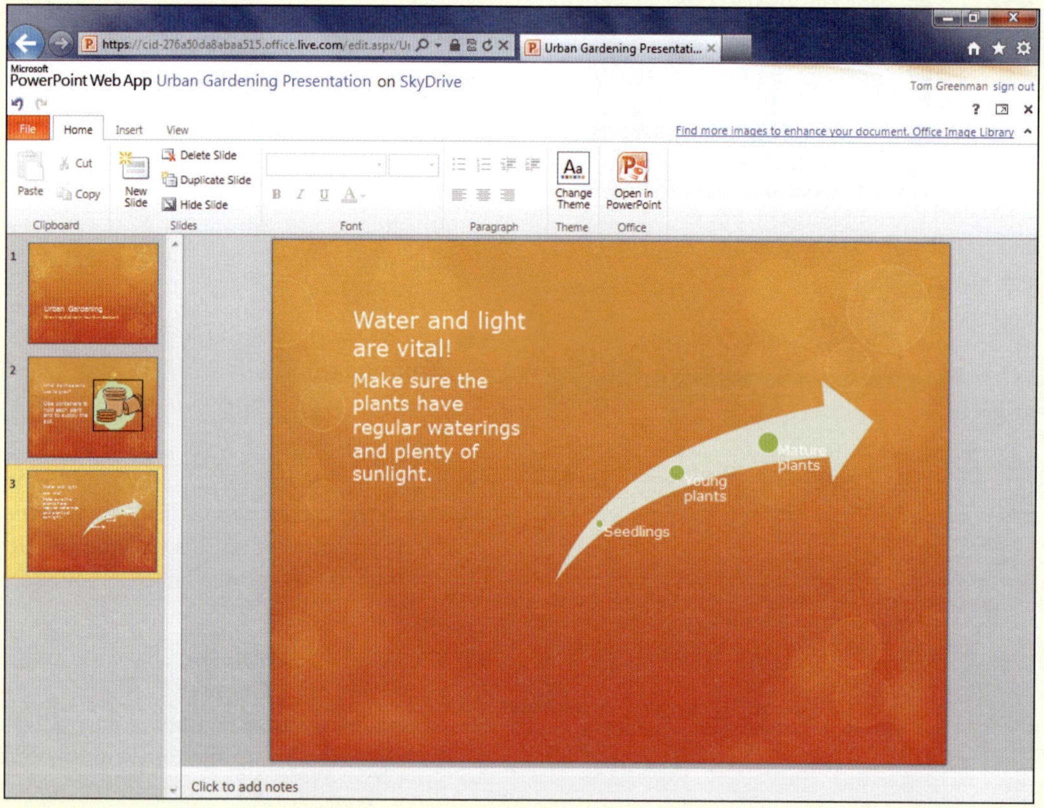

Figure 1

Skills in Context

To complete this project, you will need the following file:

- **New blank Word Web Apps document**

You will save your snip as:

- **Lastname_Firstname_wa02_Community**

The Aspen Falls Parks and Recreation Department has created a community garden space for the citizens of Aspen Falls. The garden space is free, but in return, each gardener must donate 50 percent of the vegetables they raise to the local food bank. A flyer needs to be developed that will be posted in various locations around the city to help advertise the garden space.

Using Office Web Apps, create a flyer that advertises the community garden space. Format the text so that the title stands out enough that it can be read from a distance. Insert one clip art picture or one SmartArt graphic. Size the text and the clip art so that all text can be read on one screen.

Create a **Full-screen snip**. Save the snip in your **Web Apps Chapter 2** folder as Lastname_Firstname_wa02_Community **Close** the **Snipping Tool** window. Submit the snip as directed by your instructor.

Done! You have completed Skills in Context

Skills and You

To complete this project, you will need the following file:

- **New blank PowerPoint Web App presentation**

You will save your snip as:

- **Lastname_Firstname_wa02_Favorites**

Using the skills you have practiced in this chapter, create a presentation with four slides describing three of your favorite things. Make slide 1 a title slide to introduce your favorites. The remaining slides should describe each of the favorites. Include clip art, pictures, or SmartArt graphics on at least two different slides.

Create a **Full-screen snip**. Save the snip in your **Web Apps Chapter 2** folder as Lastname_Firstname_wa02_Favorites **Close** the **Snipping Tool** window. Submit the snip as directed by your instructor.

Done! You have completed Skills and You

Glossary

AutoSum An Excel feature used to insert a prewritten function into a cell.

Breadcrumb trail A text navigation bar that shows your place in a hierarchy of web pages or nested folders or files.

CAPTCHA A test used to ensure that forms are filled in by human beings and commonly used to prevent computer programs from automating tasks such as creating Windows Live accounts.

Cell Where one column and one row intersect in an Excel worksheet.

Cell reference Identifies the cell location by listing the column first and then listing the row.

Chart A graphic representation of data.

Cloud computing An Internet technology used to store files and to work with programs that are stored in a central location.

Excel Web App The part of Office Web Apps used to work with Excel workbooks and worksheets.

Folder A unit used to organize similar or related files and information.

Formatting When bold, italic, or font color is added to a word.

Function A process that performs a mathematical calculation according to the cell references and values in their parentheses.

Hotmail A free Web-based email service provided by Microsoft.

Messenger A Windows Live instant messaging service that can be used to communicate instantly using text or web cams.

Note container Placeholders that hold the content on a OneNote page.

Office Web Apps Web-based versions of Microsoft Office programs (Word, Excel, PowerPoint, and One Note) that are available online through Windows Live.

OneNote Web App The part of Office Web Apps used to manage information such as text, images, and multimedia in one location as if you had a single notebook.

Permissions Settings that allow another person to access, read, modify, or delete files or folders.

PowerPoint Web App The part of Office Web Apps used to work with PowerPoint presentations.

Range A group of adjacent cells.

Slide An individual page or screen in a presentation that can contain text, pictures, tables, charts, and other multimedia or graphic objects.

SmartArt graphic Designer-quality visual representations of information to communicate ideas in a variety of layouts.

Snipping Tool A program included with Windows 7 that can be used to capture an image of the screen or part of the screen and then save it as a file.

Subfolder A folder inside another folder.

Theme A predefined set of colors, fonts, lines, fill effects, and graphics that are applied to your entire document, workbook, presentation, or web page.

Value A cell's data.

Windows Live A large group of cloud-based technologies including email, social networking, and applications that are accessed through a website that is used for communication, storage of files and folders, and sharing of files and folders.

Windows Live ID The email address that is your user name to log on to Windows Live.

Windows Live SkyDrive A Windows Live service used to store, access, and share files and folders.

Word Web App The word-processing application used to create documents that is available as part of Office Web Apps.

Workbook An Excel file that contains one or more worksheets.

Worksheet Used in Excel to store and work with data.

Index

CW The internet icon represents Index entries found within More Skills on the Companion Website: www.pearsonhighered.com/skills